Approaches to Data Design, Engineering, and Development

IDMA 203 COURSE STUDY GUIDE

Insurance Data Management Association (IDMA)
Associate Insurance Data Manager (AIDM)
Designation Program

Technics Publications
SEDONA, ARIZONA

Published by:

115 Linda Vista
Sedona, AZ 86336 USA
www.TechnicsPub.com

Cover design by Lorena Molinari

First Edition

First Printing 2026

ISBN, print ed.   9798898161071
ISBN, Kindle ed.   9798898161088
ISBN, PDF ed.   9798898161095

Contents

Introduction

Founded in 1983, IDMA is an independent nonprofit professional association dedicated to increasing the level of professionalism, knowledge, and visibility of insurance data management through education, research, annual forums, local chapter meetings, news bulletins, and peer-to-peer networking. It serves individuals employed in any aspect of insurance data management. This includes individuals engaged in any of the following enterprise information governance activities within various functional areas of insurance companies, regulatory bodies, statistical/rating organizations, industry consulting firms, professional associations and learned societies, and technology research and services providers:

- data definition
- data collection
- data administration
- data standards
- data processing
- data analysis
- internal and external data reporting
- data quality.

The main objective of IDMA is the administration of an educational program designed to increase professional proficiency and to provide a professional designation in the data management discipline. Additionally, IDMA provides an ongoing forum for the discussion of issues and innovations in data management through technical seminars, educational workshops, and publications.

IDMA courses, workshops, and forums are highly recommended for a broad audience including new hires, IT and data modeling professionals who want to broaden their knowledge of the business side of insurance data management, anyone who manages and governs data in the industry (statistical, or management information data), and anyone who needs to use or communicate good quality data/information – from actuaries to underwriters, and claims and analytics professionals.

Students who complete the four IDMA-developed courses and successfully pass the examinations are awarded an *Associate Insurance Data Manager (AIDM®)* designation. The IDMA courses may be taken in any order; there are no prerequisites. However, the courses are numbered to indicate a recommended sequence.

Students who complete additional course work from other selected insurance industry educational organizations and successfully pass the specified examinations receive the *Certified Insurance Data Manager (CIDM®)* designation.

For details on the designation requirements, please refer to the IDMA website at www.IDMA.org or call our office at +1 (201) 469-3069.

Using this Course Guide

This course guide will help you learn the course content and prepare for the exam.

Almost all assignments in this course guide, except for the final assignment, which is a recap of the prior assignments, include the following components:

- **Educational Objectives**. These are the most important study tools in the course guide. Because all of the questions on the exam are based on the Educational Objectives, the best way to study for the exam is to focus on these objectives.

- **Key Terms and Concepts**. These terms and concepts are fundamental to understanding the assignment. After completing the required reading, test your understanding of the assignment's Key Terms and Concepts by writing their definitions.

- **Review Questions**. The review questions test your understanding of what you have read. Review the Educational Objectives and required reading, then answer the questions to the best of your ability. When you are finished, check the answers at the end of the assignment to evaluate your comprehension.

- **Discussion Questions**. These questions are intended to continue to test your knowledge of the required reading by applying what you've studied to real-life situations. No suggested answers are provided at the end of the assignment for these types of open discussion questions. Answers may vary by student and will depend on their organization's culture, resources, and processes.

Important Note Applicable to All IDMA Course Material: IDMA strives to keep all of its course material current. The information provided is up to date at the time of publication. The timing and pace of industry changes, along with the constraints of publication, can at times result in a lag in updates being included. IDMA regularly reviews content to ensure that it is current and will publish updates as necessary and appropriate.

Exam Information

IDMA exams are given online, consist of 100 multiple-choice and true/false type questions, and are three hours long. Unofficial scores are tabulated and issued immediately after the exam completion. Official scores are mailed to students within 15 business days after the conclusion of the exam cycle. The passing score is 70%.

Students are allowed to take more than one course exam during an exam cycle. Students are also allowed to retake an exam within the same exam cycle if they were not successful on their first try.

Exams are conducted with no reference materials, papers, books, or other aids permitted in the room. No student may communicate with another during the exam. Students are not allowed to maintain copies of their exams. All exam materials are considered the property of IDMA.

Exam Registration Information and Requirements

Currently, IDMA does not contract with testing centers (such as Prometric, Pearson, and Kryterion) to host its exams onsite. IDMA exams are given, so far as possible, at the student's worksite with the cooperation of the human resources or education department in locating a proctor and site.

NOTE: Students are responsible for locating a proctor and providing IDMA with the proctor's contact information. A proctor could be anyone from your HR department, your manager, or a staffer. A week before the exam, IDMA will email your proctor a "proctor package" that explains the exam process. You will also receive your exam pass via email around the same time.

The purchase of the study guide for the current IDMA course does not automatically register a candidate for the examination. As you proceed with your studies, be sure to arrange for your exam.

- Visit our website at www.IDMA.org to access and print the exam registration form, which contains information and forms needed to register for your exam.
- Plan to register with IDMA well in advance of your exam. Late fees apply two weeks prior to the start of the exam cycle.
- Coordinate with your proctor on the exam date and start time.

How to Study for IDMA Exams

Use the assigned study materials (textbook and course guide). Focus your study on the Educational Objectives presented at the beginning of each course guide assignment. Thoroughly read the textbook and any other assigned materials, and then complete the course guide exercises. Choose a study method that best suits your needs; for example, participate in a traditional class, an informal study group, or study on your own. IDMA recommends that you begin your studies for the exam at least two months before your scheduled exam date.

Student Resources

For more information on any of the IDMA publications, course examinations, and other services:

- Visit our website at www.IDMA.org.
- Call us at +1 (201) 469-3069.

- Fax us at +1 (201) 748-1690.
- Write to us at Insurance Data Management Association (IDMA), 545 Washington Boulevard, 16th Floor, Jersey City, NJ 07310.

Modern Drivers for Data Design, Engineering, and Development

Educational Objectives

Upon completion of this assignment, you should be able to:

1. Describe the challenges faced in delivering current information technology solutions.
2. Explain how data and information have become central to business today.
3. Define the terms *data driven* and *information informed*.
4. Define *digital business/digital transformation*.
5. Describe the challenges and opportunities seen in digital business.
6. Explain the information and technological underpinnings of digital transformation.
7. Show how serious crises, such as the COVID-19 pandemic, political upheaval, or the climate emergency, may provide the impetus for change in business operations and strategy.
8. Explain the historical, current, and emerging relationship between business and IT.
9. Define the characteristics of the biz-tech ecosystem.

For each assignment, define or describe each of the Key Terms and Concepts and answer each of the Review and Discussion Questions.

Key Terms and Concepts

Informational Applications:

Digital Information System Architecture (DISA):

Information:

Creation Context:

Usage Context:

Big Data Analytics:

Data-Driven:

Information Informed:

Tactical Decisions:

Strategic Decisions:

Operational Decisions:

Digital Business:

Digital Transformation:

Innovation:

Biz-Tech Ecosystem:

Review Questions

1) Why are informational applications important to businesses and what are the long-standing issues associated with them?

2) List the troubles associated with data- and information-centric technology solutions.

3) Why is a DISA critical to today's business?

4) For designing and building data and information systems, why is it useful to use information as a starting point rather than data for discussion between business and IT departments about how to meet business needs and deliver useful and usable solutions?

5) How does traditional metadata relate to creation context?

6) What are the expectations for all information today?

7) What is information in a business context?

8) In the DISA, how are data and information distinguished and why does focusing on data rather than information matter?

9) What is the aim of data-driven businesses and how might that lead decision makers astray?

10) What is the concept of data-driven based on?

11) To become data-driven, a business must extend the concept of combining data from multiple sources beyond operational analytics to tactical and strategic decision making. What are the challenges involved?

12) How do the approaches of traditional applications and digital information systems differ?

13) What are the two critical success factors for delivering a digital information system, including a data warehouse?

14) Identify two potential agents of change that can drive the development of information systems.

15) True or False? Digital transformation is all about strategy and new ways of thinking.

16) List the five domains of digital transformation.

17) How is competition in digital business different from that in a traditional business?

18) How does a revised vision of competition support digital business transformation?

19) How does digital transformation support innovation?

20) Compare innovation through digital transformation to the pre-digital approach?

21) What is a downside to minimal viable prototypes in digital transformation innovation?

22) Describe a traditional business's understanding of value and how it changes with digital transformation.

23) How do businesses use the growing volume of Internet data to support digital transformation?

24) How has the Internet of Things (IoT) improved business operations?

25) How must internal information systems adjust to achieve the aim of digital business, the complete convergence of the real world outside of the business with the internal applications and systems within?

26) As business transformation occurs, how do business users' needs, behaviors, and roles change?

27) As a business transformation occurs, how does the role of IT change?

28) What are the concerns related to digital transformation's use of external data and data from physical sensors?

29) Global challenges such as pandemics, climate and environmental crises, social problems caused by inequality, and changing political attitudes may affect businesses more than digital transformation. What are some of the issues that could influence IT approaches more than digital transformation?

30) Which of the following statements is false of IT in reinventing the business process?
    A.   Leveraging IT is strongly correlated to enabling leading companies to change and improve their operations in fundamental ways.
    B.   IT is a catalyst for innovative ideas.

    C.   IT is an engine for delivering on innovative ideas.
    D.   Failure of IT to take a more central role in business, or of business to accept this new IT role, will not affect the success of digital transformation efforts.

31) List the fundamental behavioral changes needed across the business to facilitate the symbiotic relationship between IT and business.

32) What is IT's role in supporting the behavioral changes needed for successful digital transformation?

33) Describe how the biz-tech ecosystem provides a closed-loop to improve business success.

34) List the characteristics of a biz-tech ecosystem.

35) Which of the following is false in a biz-tech ecosystem?
    A.   When the business comes up with a new idea, their first thought is to look for a vendor to see how information technology can implement that innovation.
    B.   Similarly, IT is always looking to the business to see what future technologies can open up new opportunities or solve old problems.
    C.   Businesspeople must understand technology and IT must move away from the idea that their role is mostly or maybe entirely about technology.
    D.   Information and data must flow freely within the enterprise, between the enterprise and its customers, between different enterprises, as well as to and from regulators.

36) Identify two issues that can undermine trust in a biz-tech ecosystem.

Discussion Questions

NOTE: The questions below are intended to continue to challenge you to test your knowledge of the required reading by applying what you have studied to real-life situations.

No suggested answers are provided at the end of the assignment for these types of open discussion questions. Answers may vary by student and will depend on their organization's culture, resources, and processes.

1) Is your company in the process of developing a digital business? If so, what has led to success? What efforts have had limited success?

    Issues to consider: Leadership, reorganization efforts, need for external data, legacy systems, and skills.

2) How has your company used external data, and how has this driven digital transformation?

    Issues to consider: Operational, tactical, and strategic decision making; the types of external data needed.

3) What efforts have been made to verify the accuracy of external data? How does your company address issues related to security and privacy?

    Issues to consider: Sources of data, security and privacy procedures, data scrubbing/cleansing algorithms.

Answers to Assignment 1 Questions

NOTE: These answers are provided to give students a basic understanding of acceptable types of responses. They are often not the only valid answers and are not intended to provide an exhaustive response to the questions.

Key Terms and Concepts

Informational Applications: A subset of applications that businesspeople use and classes of problems they encounter.

Digital Information System Architecture (DISA): A multidisciplinary and multilevel approach across all business and IT functions within the organization that begins with architecture and design, extending to engineering and development, maintenance, and all the way to business use and back.

Information: Information is what people create as a means of expressing themselves and often for communicating with others.

Creation Context: Data creation occurs at a certain time and place, using specific tools, all of which may be relevant to the meaning or use of the information thus created.

Usage Context: How information is used to support management, analysis, decision making, and action taking throughout the organization.

Big Data Analytics: Analysis techniques based on the understanding that big data provides statistical and actionable insights into the behaviors, needs, and expectations of customers and prospects of largely online businesses.

Data-Driven: All decisions and processes are dictated by data.

Information Informed: Clarification of the concept of data-driven, which incorporates context.

Tactical Decisions: Medium-term decisions made by mid-level managers based on well-known and well-understood data/information.

Strategic Decisions: Long-term, high financial impact decisions made by executives, which should (ideally) be influenced by real and relevant information.

Operational Decisions: Short-term decisions made by operational managers and staff to keep the business running. Operational decisions are founded on basic data and usually have a limited financial impact.

Digital Business: The creation of new business designs by blurring the digital and physical worlds. Digital should be viewed as a way of doing things rather than a thing in itself.

Digital Transformation: Used synonymously with digital business. However, in discussing digital transformation, the discussion will veer towards technology or information.

Innovation: How new ideas emerge, are tested, and brought to market.

Biz-Tech Ecosystem: An organizational restructuring that puts business and IT on an equal footing, both focused on business goals, and both recognizing the fundamental importance of information and technology in delivering them.

Review Questions

1) These applications are information-centric and, from a business perspective, focus on delivering business information for a wide and varied set of uses. Issues relate to data/information, including its collection, creation, meaning, use, storage, management, and disposal.

2) Troubles associated with data- and information-centric technology solutions are:
   - Collecting the wrong or unneeded data for the business objectives.
   - Providing users with ill-defined information.
   - Combining data incorrectly from multiple sources.
   - Failing to reconcile data to common models, structures, and timing.
   - Delivering data at the wrong time or at the wrong speed.
   - Providing too much or too little information to meet the business needs.
   - Developing systems that struggle to respond to rapidly changing business needs.
   - Failing to provide meaningful, usable, useful, and valuable data to the business.

3) DISA provides the breadth and depth required for the extensive information systems used by today's businesses. It is particularly important to note that extensive information needs must be addressed not only in the development of new systems but also in existing environments and legacy systems that are primary data sources for many future information systems.

4) Determining which context should be added around data can be confusing. Starting the discussion with information, however, leads to more clarity.

5) Traditional metadata represents some—mostly technical—aspects of the creation context of information.

6) Today, all information, almost without exception, is digitally encoded, processed, and stored either transiently or permanently in some sort of computing or communications device. The expectation is that it will be permanently available, readable, and searchable while also secure and private as required.

7) Focusing on the business environment, information is what people (and, increasingly, artificial intelligence) use to support management, analysis, decision making, and action taking throughout the organization.

8) Data is a subset of information from which context has been stripped to a greater or lesser extent. When we focus on data rather than information, we risk misunderstanding or misinterpreting the meaning and relevance of the information from which that data was derived. Furthermore—and this becomes a central pillar of digital information solutions architecture—we need to understand where that context goes or resides when it is sucked out of information.

9) The aim is to eliminate from the business all decisions made on the basis of "gut feel," intuition, personal biases, or hidden motivations. Data without this context might lead users to make poor decisions.

10) The widespread availability of large volumes of current and historical data, combined with cheap and powerful processing, enables extensive, statistically based analytics to become the basis and driver of accurate, timely decision making.

11) At the tactical level, the need for more extensive context around data poses challenges in using data correctly and to its full extent. At the strategic level, the requirement for information rather than data adds more significant issues. In addition, at both these levels, being unconditionally *driven* by anything leaves little or no room for human judgment, social ethics, or basic flexibility in decision making. Decisions informed by contextually rich information—information informed—intuitively offer a seemingly better route to valuable decisions.

12) The approaches of traditional applications and digital information systems differ:
   - Where traditional applications typically focus first on function and action, and then the data needed to support that function, digital information systems more often begin with data/information capable of supporting multiple functions, decisions, and actions.
   - The characteristics of a digital information system, with its focus on data/information to support multiple functions, do not align well with a traditional project-focused development approach. Rather, they demand a program approach consisting of a rolling set of projects.

13) The two critical success factors to delivering a digital information system, including a data warehouse, are:
   - Organizational structure focused on the relationship between the business and IT functions within the organization and who in the C-suite is driving the program.
   - The need for a powerful, cross-functional agent of change that motivates much or all of the organization to undertake and persevere with the program.

14) The two potential agents of change that can drive the development of information systems are:
   - An agreed, companywide, long-term business and technology strategic direction, often with the self-imposed goal of reinventing the business.
   - A sudden, extreme crisis of unexpected proportions that drives major disruption in the social, environmental, and financial environment in which the business and, indeed, its customers and competitors operate.

15) The statement is True.

16) The five domains of digital transformation are:
   - Customers
   - Competition
   - Innovation
   - Value
   - Data.

17) Competition in a digital world replaces rivalry between similar businesses within an industry with a mix of cooperation and disintermediation (the removal of intermediaries), and novel forms of digitally based asymmetric competition across increasingly fluid industry boundaries.

18) Platform business models can allow one business to dominate (winner takes all) a particular market due to network effects. The net effect is a move from zero-sum competition between traditional and similar rivals to competing with firms with very dissimilar business models "invading" the traditional market and serving the ultimate customer in different ways.

19) Digital transformation offers the opportunity for continuous learning and rapid experimentation using data models and, in the extreme, digital twins (in-depth, real-time digital models/replicas of real-world entities, including devices and machines, people, and organizational entities such as cities) to gain market feedback at the earliest possible moment without investing in physical prototyping and building full-function initial products.

20) In the pre-digital era, innovation sprang mainly from product managers' intuition, and the cost of failure was often high. The digital approach relies on minimum viable prototypes (MVPs) and maximum learning in the customer environment.

21) MVPs may introduce unforeseen problems in "non-functional" aspects such as security and privacy, and include undiscovered bugs that necessitate multiple, rapid upgrades impacting customer satisfaction and value.

22) Traditionally, a firm's basic value proposition remained relatively constant over the years, and a successful firm could demonstrate a clear value proposition, market differentiation, and a focus on executing and delivering the best version year after year. The rapid evolution of customer needs and the competitive environment, driven by digital transformation, forces businesses to continually refine customer value and adapt early to market indicators to stay ahead of the curve.

23) Businesses can use the extensive data on what people are interested in from Internet searches and social media to create powerful, compelling stories about prospects and customers. Wide-ranging analytics and artificial intelligence augment human decision making and enable predictions of future behavior, as well as increase the ability to influence and manipulate those behaviors in real time.

24) The detailed, continuous streams of sensor data provided by the IoT, which build comprehensive views and histories of physical events and environmental measures, enable the automation of industrial processes, the optimization of smart cities, and the proliferation of autonomous vehicles.

25) Internal information systems must accommodate pervasive data/information in multiple forms and locations, as well as provide universal access to and use of it through extensive analytics and artificial intelligence/machine learning algorithms.

26) As a business transformation occurs, the business users' needs, behaviors, and roles change:
- At the beginning of the process, the user selects metrics from operational systems to manage and monitor business measures.
- Later, business users need descriptive decision support focusing on describing past business performance, comparing it to expectations or plans, and taking corrective action.
- Further along the evolution, business users use predictive analytics to discover and act on insights. Data scientists bypass IT, going directly to the data.
- In a fully digital business, business analysts rely on predictive and prescriptive activity trying to influence (or manipulate) future behavior of people or physical outcomes. Artificial intelligence and machine learning have become the tools of choice.

27) As a business transformation occurs the role of IT changes:
- Before digital transformation, IT provides metrics from operational systems to support managing and monitoring of business activity.
- Later, IT is tasked with providing descriptive metrics to enable the business to compare current performance with past performance.
- As digital transformation continues to evolve, IT is forced to adapt continuously to changing information resources and uses, integrating data and information from all potential sources across multiple platforms.

28) Information/data purchased from businesses that collect data specifically or repurpose their own data for sale may raise privacy, quality, or other concerns. Even data gathered from an enterprise's own physical sensor infrastructure may come with quality issues, such as corrupted or missing data values, or risk of manipulation as it passes through the public Internet.

29) Some issues that could influence IT approaches more than digital transformation include:
- **Distance is back**: Global supply chains, just-in-time products, and cross-border travel become less attractive.
- **Resilience and efficiency**: The ability to absorb a shock and recover quickly is becoming as important as cost and efficiency, affecting global supply chains, management succession plans, etc.
- **The rise of the contact-free economy**: Digital commerce, telemedicine, and general automation trends could accelerate and become irreversible.
- **Changing business environment**: As industry structures, consumer behavior, market positions, and sector attractiveness adjust to a new normal, businesses must define new strategies and adopt new behaviors.
- **Finding the silver linings**: Changes to existing processes and ways of working, driven by necessity, show what can be changed or reinvented—doing more with less, simplifying processes, and speeding up decisions.

30) The correct answer choice is D.

Here is a list of the fundamental behavioral changes needed across the business to facilitate the symbiotic relationship between IT and business:
- Reposition information from the periphery to the core of decision making at all levels.
- Use information from all sources—internal and external—with proper confidence in its quality.
- Supplement and replace as appropriate scheduled activities with real-time, on-demand action.
- Adapt continuously to unexpected change with agility and speed.
- Adopt closed-loop decision-making and action-taking processes.
- Collaborate across business functions, geographies, and enterprise boundaries.
- Adopt mobile and remote interaction and working as the norm.

32) It is the role and responsibility of IT to discover and understand the potential benefits and challenges of emerging technologies within the business context, work collaboratively with the business to promote new tools as appropriate, and deliver them as needed.

33) The biz-tech ecosystem provides a closed-loop to improve business success:
- Business is under pressure from the level of change and uncertainty in the external market and from competition, all of which are driving it to change and behave differently.

- Improved availability and variety of external information help the business handle these pressures and decide the best course of action.
- IT and business collaborate to develop solutions to leverage new sources of information.
- IT delivers systems to facilitate customer interactions through mobile and remote interactions.
- The customer information provided to the business through IT serves as the basis for faster decision-making and more appropriate action-taking within the business.

34) The characteristics of a biz-tech ecosystem are:
- Reintegration of the different technology stacks that exist in most enterprises, as well as the reintegration of the organizations and departments that exist across the business, with the goal of improved, seamless communication.
- Interdependence of business and IT, with the aim of creating a classical positive feedback loop between both parties.
- Crossover between business and IT skills.
- Cooperation within a biz-tech ecosystem and across its boundaries.
- Trust both within the organization and beyond its boundaries.

35) The correct answer choice is A.

36) Two issues that can undermine trust in a biz-tech ecosystem are:
- Pervasive Internet and social technologies can create or destroy trust across enterprise boundaries, so the intentions and motivations of the interacting parties must be defined and documented as part of the process.
- An increasing threat to trust is the growth of hyper-competition—competition for its own sake—rather than for the good of the competing parties, their customers, and society at large.

Frameworks for Business-IT Collaboration

Educational Objectives

Upon completion of this assignment, you should be able to:

1. Explain the purpose and content of a corporate or enterprise strategy.
2. Describe what is meant by a data/information strategy and why it is an important part of enterprise strategy for digital transformation.
3. Position the digital information systems strategy in relation to the data/information strategy and to subsequent architecture definition.
4. Define and give examples of an enterprise architecture.
5. Define conceptual architecture and its role in a digital information systems strategy.
6. Provide an overview of the meaning of a Digital Information Systems Architecture (DISA).
7. Position the conceptual, logical, and physical architecture levels of a DISA.
8. Explain the acronym IDEAL as applied to the DISA conceptual architecture and list its characteristics.
9. Define the three thinking spaces of the IDEAL architecture.
10. Explain its benefits and challenges, as well as the business value it delivers.
11. Describe the three axes of the information thinking space and explain their importance.
12. Explain how the IDEAL information architecture provides a foundation for quality work by an Insurance Data Manager.

For each assignment, define or describe each of the Key Terms and Concepts and answer each of the Review and Discussion Questions.

Key Terms and Concepts

Strategy:

Corporate or Enterprise Strategy:

Data Strategy:

Supra-Enterprise Information Model:

Thinking Space:

Enterprise Architecture:

Conceptual Architecture:

Digital Information Systems Architecture (DISA):

Emergence:

The IDEAL Information Space:

Review Questions

1) List the four criteria of an effective strategy.

2) Identify the components of an enterprise strategy.

3) What are common approaches to an industry analysis?

4) Although the stages of evolution and associated principles seem obvious, what are some concerns for implementation of a strategy for an insurance business?

5) Describe the four characteristics of data, a unique organizational asset.

6) Digital information systems strategy considers both process and people who support information. List the actions applied to information that are included in processes.

7) Digital information systems strategy considers both process and people who support information. Identify what needs to be considered with respect to people in the digital information system strategy.

8) Identify the five postulates of digital information systems.

9) John Zachman's works provide an understanding of the questions that need to be asked in developing an enterprise architecture. List the six classifications he introduced.

10) The Zachman Framework crossed the six classifications of questions to ask when developing an enterprise architecture with six levels of scope or audience perspective (roles). List these roles.

11) How can the Zachman Framework be simplified to a three-level approach to DISA?

12) Describe The Open Group Architecture Framework (TOGAF) for enterprise architecture.

13) Compare the Zachman Framework and TOGAF.

14) Identify two criticisms of traditional enterprise architecture.

15) Why could an external view of the business improve an enterprise architecture?

16) Identify the building blocks of conceptual architecture.

17) Identify the axes for each thinking space of the conceptual architecture presented in the text.

18) The term IDEAL was chosen to emphasize that the conceptual architecture is never perfected. Why not?

19) Identify and describe the five key characteristics of the IDEAL architecture.

20) Identify and describe five important additional characteristics of the IDEAL conceptual architecture.

21) Identify the benefits of the IDEAL architecture.

22) Identify the challenges of defining and implementing an IDEAL architecture.

23) Identify the ways in which implementing an IDEAL conceptual architecture drives digital business value.

24) Identify the three DISA Information Space axes and list classes for each.

25) The Reliance/Usage (RU) Axis of the DISA Information Space shows the level of trust that the business can place in information and how safely it can be used. Identify the characteristics of the axis.

26) While telematic information is useful, calculating and continually adjusting premiums requires data from traditional operational systems. How are these types of information classified on the three axes of the DISA Information Space?

27) Identify some of the issues Insurance Data Managers face in managing the ever-increasing amount of externally sourced data.

28) How does the DISA Information Space help Insurance Data Managers manage the increasing volume of data/information?

Discussion Questions

NOTE: The questions below are intended to continue to challenge you to test your knowledge of the required reading by applying what you have studied to real-life situations.

No suggested answers are provided at the end of the assignment for these types of open discussion questions. Answers may vary by student and will depend on their organization's culture, resources, and processes.

1) Using the Zachman Framework, discuss how someone in your role might describe your answers to the key questions.

2) Discuss how various types of data used in marketing would fit into the DISA Information Space.

Answers to Assignment 2 Questions

NOTE: These answers are provided to give students a basic understanding of acceptable types of responses. They are often not the only valid answers and are not intended to provide an exhaustive response to the questions.

Key Terms and Concepts

Strategy: The highest-level guidance available to an organization, focusing activities on articulated goal achievement and providing direction and specific guidance when faced with a stream of decisions or uncertainties.

Corporate or Enterprise Strategy: The top-level strategy applying to the entire organization.

Data Strategy: The highest level of guidance available to an organization, focusing data-related activities on articulated data goal achievements and providing directional and specific guidance when faced with a stream of decisions or uncertainties about organizational data assets and their application toward business objectives.

Supra-Enterprise Information Model: A comprehensive information model that spans all intra- and inter-enterprise activities, taking into account that no person or organization is an island, that we are all interconnected, and the actions of one influence those of another.

Thinking Space: Conceptual area designed first as a pause for thought, an opportunity for increased communication within the business and within IT, and between business and IT.

Enterprise Architecture: A rigorous description of the structure of an enterprise comprised of enterprise components (business entities), the externally visible properties of those components, and the relationships (the behavior) between them.

Conceptual Architecture: Provides a shared structure and vocabulary to allow business and IT to discuss and settle on business drivers and information technology enablers.

Digital Information Systems Architecture (DISA): Provides an information-focused architectural model that is simpler than the enterprise architecture model and is more appropriate for data management professionals as a basis for discussion of data design, engineering, and development issues.

Emergence: From the mathematical field of chaos theory, a process where interactions among smaller or simpler entities give rise to larger entities that exhibit complex properties absent at the individual level.

The IDEAL Information Space: A conceptual view of the entire information resource of the enterprise—whatever its source, structure, or storage—that the business uses or may use to achieve its goals.

Review Questions

1) The four criteria of an effective strategy are:
   - Express specific goals.
   - Delineate a specific scope.
   - Describe the advantage sought.
   - Articulate why the strategy is achievable.

2) The components of an enterprise strategy are
   - Industry analysis.
   - Long-term planning.
   - Core competences.
   - Financial structure.

3) Common approaches to an industry analysis include:
   - Competition within the industry.
   - Potential of new entrants.
   - Power of suppliers.
   - Power of customers.
   - Threat of substitute products.
   - PESTLE analysis - political, economic, socio-cultural, technological, legal, and environmental factors.

4) Some concerns for the implementation of a strategy for an insurance business are:
   - The level and location of the required investment.
   - Introducing and nurturing a digital culture across the entire organization.
   - The cultural and behavioral change needed across the entire business organization, especially IT, which becomes pivotal to implementing a digital business.

5) The four characteristics of data are:
   - **Non-depletable**: Data can be reused many times without losing value.
   - **Non-degrading**: Unlike other assets, data assets do not degrade over time (provided they are properly maintained).
   - **Durable**: Capable of generating flows of goods and services over time.
   - **Strategic**: Critical to the future of the organization.

6) The actions applied to information that are included in processes are:
   - Create or collect.
   - Communicate.
   - Store or dispose of.
   - Cleanse, reconcile, or manipulate in any way.
   - Present or visualize to humans.

7) With respect to people, the following need to be considered in the digital information system strategy:
   - What motivates and drives people.
   - How people make decisions.

- How people interact, both formally and informally.
- How organizational units at all levels, both formal and informal, behave.
- The methodologies they develop to run and manage the business.
- How people use information—inadvertently or deliberately—to misinterpret, obstruct, or corrupt the goals of the business.

8) The five postulates of digital information systems are:
- The information/action continuum: A seamless, closed-loop continuum from information and derived insights through decision making to action taking and back is fundamental to digital business.
- An integrated, coherent information asset: An information thinking space that represents all the information of every type used within and beyond the business is required.
- Managed, minimal duplicate information: Ideally, the information space is best maintained as a single copy of each entity.
- An integrated, closed-loop process environment: A process thinking space that is model-based, planned, and delivered in a consistent and integrated manner.
- An adaptive, flexible people milieu: A people thinking space must be highly flexible in today's ever-changing environment and be aware of the roles of people within all their activities.

9) The six classifications John Zachman introduced are:
- **What**: Things important to the business, inventory sets, and data (or better information).
- **How**: Processes the business performs, process flows, and functions.
- **Where**: Locations where the business operates, distribution networks.
- **Who**: Organizations/agents important to the business, responsibility assignments (roles), and people.
- **When**: Events significant to the business, timing cycles.
- **Why**: Business goals and strategy, motivation, and intentions.

10) John Zachman introduced the following six roles:
- Scope contexts/Executive perspective.
- Business concepts/Business management perspective.
- System logic/Architect perspective.
- Technology physics/Engineer perspective.
- Tool components/Technician perspective.
- Operation instances/Enterprise (users) perspective, usually not formally considered as part of an enterprise architecture, but worth considering as the endpoint of all this effort.

11) The Zachman Framework can be simplified to a three-level approach to DISA:
- **Conceptual**: Combining the top three (Executive, Business Management, and Architect) perspectives to provide a shared structure and vocabulary to discuss and agree on business drivers and information technology enablers between business and IT.
- **Logical**: Corresponding to the Architect and Engineer perspectives to design the functional components—largely technological in nature, but also organizational or methodological as appropriate—needed to deliver the conceptual architecture.
- **Physical**: Corresponding to the Technician perspective, to select appropriate tools and platforms to deliver the functions described at the logical level.

12) TOGAF offers a comprehensive, evolving approach to enterprise architecture, as well as a methodology for design, planning, implementation, and governance. TOGAF is structured into four domains: Business, Application, Data, and Technology architectures.

13) The Zachman Framework has six roles, while TOGAF has four domains. Both provide a structure for conceiving and envisioning an enterprise architecture. The Zachman Framework is an elegant, comprehensive structure. TOGAF provides a more comprehensive methodology for design, planning, implementation, and governance.

14) Traditional enterprise architectures focus too strongly on the internals of the enterprise and accept some important current conditions, such as existing business goals, strategies, and rules, with little questioning.

15) External influences on the enterprise are numerous and may be particularly intense. In a digital business, significant volumes of data—also exhibiting high velocity and extensive variability—are exchanged between the enterprise and its external environment.

16) The building blocks of conceptual architecture are:
- Information is the foundational level.
- Process is the second block.
- People are the top block.

17) The axes for each thinking space of the conceptual architecture, as presented in the text, are:
- **People**: Roles, motivations, and attitudes.
- **Process**: Time span, business effect, and active scope.
- **Information**: Reliance/usage, timeliness/consistency, and structure/content.

18) Business and IT trade-offs are always necessary. In a constantly changing environment, business needs and technical possibilities are always evolving, and an architecture must accommodate such evolution. The conceptual architecture is therefore more an image of what we may aim to achieve rather than what can be fully delivered.

19) The five key characteristics of the IDEAL architecture include:
- **Integrated/Inclusive**: Within and across all three thinking spaces, a unity of thought and purpose drives the approach; all aspects of this architecture link and work seamlessly together and all elements of information, process, and people are included.
- **Distributed**: Each thinking space has diverse attributes of equal importance, independently implemented but mutually dependent in action. They must be implemented in a fully dispersed manner; there is no single, central control point.
- **Emergent**: Modern information processing is a chaotic/complex (mathematically and socially) environment in which all characteristics cannot be known or predicted in advance. Order materializes from the disordered; coherent structure and behavior emerge.
- **Adaptive**: As business needs and technological possibilities change, the architecture is sufficiently agile to adjust to and take advantage of them without extensive re-architecting.
- **Latent**: (Another word for hidden), this architecture is not to be explicitly implemented; it guides business and IT thinking and discussion about what is desired and possible.

20) Five important additional characteristics of the IDEAL conceptual architecture include:
- **Elegantly simple**: The picture is simple enough to be understood by both business and IT and elegant enough to enable coherent discussion of the possible consequences of actions and designs under consideration.
- **Complete**: Although impossible to prove, the architecture aims to fully describe all aspects of digital transformation that drive thinking about how it can be designed and delivered.
- **Open-system**: In contrast to the closed system thinking of many IT architectures, the IDEAL architecture crosses the enterprise boundaries to include all relevant aspects of the external world—customers, prospects, partners, regulators, government, society, and environmental factors—within which the business operates, by which it is influenced, and intends to influence in turn.
- **Enterprise-wide**: The architecture is most effective—and perhaps can only be effective at all—when applied across the entire scope of the activities of the enterprise.
- **Non-proliferating**: Encouraging a single, unique copy of each piece of information and a single version of each process instance are key visions of their respective spaces to reduce complexity and corpulence in the management of the digital business environment.

21) The benefits of the IDEAL architecture are:
- All forms of information and data, regardless of their sources or structures, fall within the scope of the architecture and can be included in business processes.
- Allows businesspeople to be more flexible and agile in their use of information and to "flow" between different types of activities—traditionally separated into operational, informational, and collaborative.
- It also offers managed support for processes being defined or modified by businesspeople—not just IT—as they increasingly create and modify workflows and define and implement activities that suit their specific needs.
- By reducing the duplication of information and its cost in the face of ever-growing information volumes, it also reduces delays in moving, copying, and/or transforming data between multiple stores, allowing businesses to operate closer to real time when needed.
- By including people's needs and behaviors as part of this architecture, we can start explicitly modeling both to represent what businesspeople are actually doing so that flexible process definitions and agile information collection and management can be driven into those processes.

22) The challenges of defining and implementing an IDEAL architecture include:
- Buy-in from the business is mandatory.
- Implementation must be driven from the CEO level.
- Integration and reintegration require breaking down organizational silos in both business and IT.
- Project management at an extremely wide scope needs to learn lessons and borrow tools from massive, successful engineering projects.

23) Implementing an IDEAL conceptual architecture drives digital business value in the following ways:
- Allows the creation and implementation of previously impossible analyses and enables improved, timely decisions based on just-in-time data and information.
- Improving the quality and consistency of information from all sources reduces confusion and misunderstanding, with direct bottom-line impacts.
- The shift from ad-hoc activities to fully managed, agile, end-to-end processes improves business efficiency, reliability, and flexibility.

- Allows the business to innovate in process creation and update, leading to improved value and return on investment.
- Can reduce the amount of information stored and manipulated, as well as the level of rework and data manipulation as it moves from original sources to its ultimate business uses, thereby reducing IT infrastructure development and maintenance costs.
- By taking a fully inclusive view of both the enterprise and its external environment, the business can properly incorporate customer, societal, and environmental good in all its behaviors.

24) The three DISA Information Space axes and their respective classes are:
- **The Timeliness/Consistency (TC) Axis**: Inflight, Live, Stable, Reconciled, and Historical.
- **The Structure/Context (SC) Axis**: Raw, Atomic, Derived, Compound, and Textual, Multiplex.
- **The Reliance/Usage (RU) Axis**: Universal, Global, Enterprise, Local, Personal, Vague, and Unknown.

25) The characteristics of the Reliance/Usage (RU) Axis of the DISA Information Space are:
- The classes on this axis range from completely trustworthy, universally usable information to information of unknown provenance that can only be used with great care.
- Enterprise information, for example, in a data warehouse, can be used across the entire organization.
- Global information can be shared with other organizations or regulators.
- Personal information (in spreadsheets, not to be confused with personally identifiable information) and vague information, such as that from YouTube, require careful identification, management, and possibly restricted access within the enterprise.

26) Data from traditional operational systems are classified on the three axes of the DISA Information Space in the following ways:
- Stable/Reconciled on the Timeliness/Consistency Axis.
- Atomic/Derived on the Structure/Context Axis.
- Enterprise/Local on the Reliance/Usage Axis.

27) In managing the ever-increasing amount of externally sourced data, Insurance Data Managers face the following issues:
- Raw data can be missing or corrupted by sensor failure, intermittent connectivity, hacking, etc.
- Data provided that a data provisioning platform provider needs a service agreement to define responsibilities and ensure data quality.
- Textual or multiplex information (audio, images, and video) has issues of context and meaning that must be resolved before combining it with internally sourced information.
- Social media data can be especially problematic. Text context can be difficult to interpret, while images and videos can be manipulated, perhaps fraudulently.
- Data/information destined for industry or governmental regulators created in spreadsheets by businesspeople on their PCs.

28) Using the information space, a Data Manager can routinely and simply examine existing or emerging data to help determine the best approach to control and manage issues related to data quality and procedures.

A Foundation for Data Solution Design

Educational Objectives

Upon completion of this assignment, you should be able to:

1. Explain the concept of information pillars.
2. Describe the three canonical pillar types: process-mediated data, machine-generated data, and human-sourced information, and their significance in data management.
3. Discuss the sources of all enterprise information/data: measures, events, and messages.
4. Explain the meaning and importance of transactions as the legally binding representation of a business' core activities.
5. Define context-setting information (CSI) and explain its relationship to metadata.
6. Describe the content of CSI via its six interrogatives, its uses, purposes, and sources.
7. Position process with respect to information and people conceptually.
8. Define and describe the three information preparation processes and their importance to data management.
9. Explain the purpose and meaning of the REAL, logical architecture.
10. Describe how the REAL, logical architecture differs from architectural patterns.
11. Discuss other considerations for DISA.
12. Explain the importance of data standards and a common data model for structuring data for shared use and business value.

For each assignment, define or describe each of the Key Terms and Concepts and answer each of the Review and Discussion Questions.

Key Terms and Concepts

Process-Mediated Data (PMD):

Machine-Generated Data (MGD):

Human-Sourced Information (HSI):

Pillar:

Transaction:

Context-Setting Information (CSI):

Information Preparation:

Instantiation:

Assimilation:

Reification:

Architectural Patterns:

Silos:

Review Questions

1) Provide insurance-related examples of the three types of data/information.

2) What determines whether telematic data is process-mediated data (PMD) or machine-generated data (MGD)?

3) Policy documents are considered human-sourced information, but may be built on machine-generated data, such as premium calculations. How does one distinguish between the two?

4) Describe the representation of classes of data/information in the logical DISA pillar.

5) Identify the key understandings of transaction when applied in the logical DISA.

6) Why does the process-mediated pillar (PMD) of the logical DISA require close attention from data managers?

7) Why should the data manager's view of the three pillars of the logical DISA extend beyond the enterprise's IT systems?

8) Social media is considered part of human-sourced information. How are data management and governance approaches handled when the business uses such data from an external provider?

9) An automobile insurance customer has a telematic device in her car. Identify where this customer's data/information would reside in the insurer's systems.

10) Identify the issues related to implementing metadata.

11) How does context-setting information support the DISA thinking spaces of information, people, and process?

12) How does CSI reflect the concerns raised in the Zachman Framework for Enterprise Architecture?

13) Identify the benefits of using context-setting questions for the exploration of CSI across all three IDEAL thinking spaces.

14) Given that context-setting information spans all three data/information pillars, what is the role of the data manager?

15) An earlier assignment in this course identified five categories of metadata: Business, Technical, Operational, Process, and Data Stewardship. How does context-setting information (CSI) relate to these categories?

16) List and describe the three processes of information preparation.

17) Which one of the following is NOT a form of instantiation?
   A. Immediate capture.
   B. Change capture.
   C. Normal capture.
   D. None of the above.

18) Identify some instantiation concerns for data managers.

19) Identify the two components of assimilation, a process of information preparation.

20) Identify the assimilation concern for data managers.

21) Explain why reification, a process of information preparation, is necessary.

22) Identify the types of tools for reification.

23) Identify the reification concern for data managers.

24) Identify and define the terms expressed in the acronym REAL, logical architecture.

25) Identify the additional components of the REAL, logical architecture that surround the information pillars (PMD, MGD, and HSI) and information preparation functions (instantiation, assimilation, and reification).

26) Identify a concern for data managers regarding the utilization component of the REAL, logical architecture.

27) What should an insurance data manager understand about emerging architectures and architectural patterns?

28) How does the DISA architecture differ from more traditional approaches?

29) Identify issues with most data warehouse architecture approaches?

30) Identify the concerns that will influence decisions on where data is stored: on premises, in the Cloud, or in some hybrid configuration.

31) Identify the important characteristics of an enterprise data model (EDM) for ensuring consistency across different data and information stores.

Discussion Questions

NOTE: The questions below are intended to continue to challenge you to test your knowledge of the required reading by applying what you have studied to real-life situations.

No suggested answers are provided at the end of the assignment for these types of open discussion questions. Answers may vary by student and will depend on their organization's culture, resources, and processes.

1) Does your company collect and use telematic data? If so, how is it used and where is it stored? What issues have you encountered with its quality and usability?

2) Describe how your company's systems support instantiation, assimilation, and reification.

Answers to Assignment 3 Questions

NOTE: These answers are provided to give students a basic understanding of acceptable types of responses. They are often not the only valid answers and are not intended to provide an exhaustive response to the questions.

Key Terms and Concepts

Process-Mediated Data (PMD): Data whose collection or creation has been strictly managed in the input process.

Machine-Generated Data (MGD): Data generated by machines, e.g., in manufacturing processes, from ATMs and the Internet of Things.

Human-Sourced Information (HSI): Information (not data) created by humans, e.g., tweets, photos, videos, and hand-drawn diagrams used for claims handling, as well as online chats or emails with claimants.

Pillar: In drawing the logical level DISA, each class of data/information is represented by a column of data/information that displays a similar set of characteristics, such that an initial high-level design choice would be to store and manage them in a similar manner, using similar technology, and perhaps even physically collocated.

Transaction: A legally binding record of some action of significance to the enterprise.

Context-Setting Information (CSI): As a replacement for metadata, provides all the background required by business and IT for each piece of information, for every process component, and for all the people—the three DISA thinking spaces—that constitute the business.

Information Preparation: The set of processes that gathers the outputs of real-world activities—events, measures, and messages—converts them into usable and useful information, and makes it available to the business as a foundation for decisions and actions taken by (or on behalf of) business people.

Instantiation: The processes by which measures, events, and messages are represented as instances of information within the pillars of the enterprise information environment.

Assimilation: The creation of derived and reconciled/consistent information sets and the creation or use of context-setting information in so doing, often across pillars.

Reification: The provision of a consistent, cross-pillar view of information according to an overarching model and access to it in real-time.

Architectural Patterns: Diagrams drawn by software product vendors, systems integrators, and/or analyst firms that describe "architecture" pictures. Such diagrams may not be what they seem and may be better described as architectural patterns rather than formal architectures.

Silos: An architectural design that creates mismatched and inconsistent sets of data used for different purposes.

Review Questions

1) Insurance-related examples of the three types of data/information are:
   - Process-mediated data (PMD) includes policyholder information from policy documents, claim settlement information, rating data from external organizations, credit scores, and data entered via online applications to obtain premium quotes.
   - Machine-generated data (MGD) includes raw telematic data collected directly by the insurer.
   - Human-sourced information (HSI) includes photos, videos, hand-drawn diagrams used for claims handling, online chats or emails with claimants, and insurance policy documents.

2) How telematic data arrives in an insurance company determines whether it is PMD or MGD. If a third-party provider has pre-processed the raw telematic data, the resulting cleansed and (possibly) summarized data passed to the insurer is properly considered and treated as process-mediated data. Only if the insurer is receiving the raw telematic data directly is it MGD.

3) The distinction revolves around the uses made of the different parts of the document. The textual content or HSI sets the human-interpretable context—that may be argued later in a court of law—of the policy; the insurance processes use the process-mediated data to bill premiums, calculate discounts, and so on.

4) Each pillar represents one of the data/information classes (PMD, MGD, HSI). Data/information in a pillar displays a similar set of characteristics, such that an initial high-level design choice would be to store and manage them in a similar manner, using similar technology, and perhaps even physically collocated. Data and information flow upwards in the pillar according to the convention that puts people at the top of the picture, as in the conceptual architecture.

5) The key understandings of transaction when applied in the logical DISA are:
   - Real-world actions are converted into transactions when they arrive at the process-mediated pillar.
   - A transaction has a different meaning from its use in database technology.
   - A transaction in the logical DISA relates to the legal status of the data/information as a complete and permanent record of a business event, as it is currently understood and agreed.

6) The creation of transactions requires proper governance and strict management, as the PMD thus created serves as the basis for the business's financial and legal obligations.

7) The data manager's view of the three pillars of the logical DISA should extend beyond the enterprise's IT systems because:
   - At the physical level, some of the enterprise's information may reside in the Cloud, leading to different management and governance approaches than those applied to on-premises storage.
   - Some of the information used by the enterprise may belong to another organization and can only be accessed as needed by the enterprise.

8) Data management and governance approaches should be based on contractual service delivery agreements between the enterprise and the social media provider.

9) For an automobile insurance customer's telematic data:
   - Personal details, existing contract details, and payment and claims history are stored in the PMD.
   - The text of her policies is stored in the HSI.
   - Events (beginning and end of driving) and measures (speed, locations, etc.) are recorded in MGD, assuming the insurer records the data directly.

10) The issues related to implementing metadata are:
   - Initially, IT defined metadata based on the technical characteristics of data, while the business preferred their own definitions for familiar data, without recognizing the value of technical specifications or cross-enterprise definitions. Without support from business projects, enterprise metadata projects failed.
   - More recently, national security agencies began using the term to refer to "envelope data" that encloses the content of phone calls, messages, and emails as a means of avoiding privacy concerns or legislation. This use of the term metadata added confusion to the meaning and potential usefulness.

11) Context-setting information (CSI) provides all the background required by business and IT for each piece of information, for every process component, and for all the people—the three DISA thinking spaces—that constitute the business.

12) The same contextual information at the micro level of information is needed at the macro level of the enterprise: what, how, where, who, when, and why. CSI is required from the same audience perspectives seen in the rows of the Zachman framework: executive, business management, architect, engineer, technician, and enterprise.

13) The benefits of using context-setting questions for the exploration of CSI across all three IDEAL thinking spaces are:
   - Promotes understanding of the linked meanings between people, process, and information.
   - Illustrates the comprehensive nature of CSI and the limitations in thinking caused by calling it metadata.

14) For a data manager, the task is to identify and correlate data/information across multiple systems and departments, irrespective of whether it is classed as operational data, content, metadata, or CSI. Proper governance must span all aspects, whether in different stores or owned by different departments.

15) CSI (or metadata) is also categorized according to its use and purpose. These categories should be considered as guidance for thinking rather than hard-and-fast rules about what they contain.
   - **Organization structures and collaborative networks**: Role-based use of information, sources of expertise.
   - **Security systems**: Access to information subsets.

16) The three processes of information preparation are:
   - **Instantiation**: The processes by which measures, events, and messages are represented as instances of information within the pillars of the enterprise information environment.
   - **Assimilation**: The creation of derived and reconciled/consistent information sets and the creation or use of context-setting information in so doing, often across pillars.

- **Reification:** The provision of a consistent, cross-pillar view of information according to an overarching model and access to it in real-time.

17) The correct answer choice is C.

18) Instantiation concerns for data managers include:
- Data acquisition may be embedded in many systems and tools.
- Some implementations driven by business are beyond the control of IT department.
- Bulk capture, the most used informally, should be monitored closely.

19) The two components of assimilation, a process of information preparation, are:
- Derivation, as the name implies, creates new information directly from an already instantiated source.
- Reconciliation and cleansing of information apply rules to information sets, often from different sources, to ensure quality and consistency.

20) For the data manager, understanding where and how assimilation is implemented is particularly important, since quality gains in the information preparation instantiation phase can be easily lost due to poor understanding or poor programming in assimilation.

21) Reification, a process of information preparation, is necessary because:
- Information resides in multiple storage technologies, so a variety of access methods are required to retrieve and convert data to a common form.
- When information must be joined for specific business needs across multiple storage technologies, a mediating layer is required to perform semantic interpretation and matching, schema translation, and so on.
- Real-time information may not be available in the derived/reconciled informational systems, necessitating real-time joins with the underlying operational systems transactions, particularly in the PMD pillar.

22) Tools are variously called data virtualization, data federation, and enterprise information integration (EII), with the exact scope and meaning of these terms often differing from vendor to vendor.

23) Unlike instantiation and assimilation, where results are stored before business gets access, in reification, the business will likely be the first to identify quality issues. Therefore, data managers must be closely involved in the design of the reification function and the models used to join data.

24) The terms expressed in the acronym REAL are:
- **Realistic:** Implementing this architecture can begin today with existing technology, and its full, foreseen extent is achievable with tools and techniques expected within a relatively short timeframe.
- **Extensible:** Given the early stage of emergence of digital business and the concepts of the biz-tech ecosystem, the functions and features are open to extension and expansion to allow expected technology evolution.
- **Actionable:** The actions and approaches required of the business and IT are clearly identified at a high level and can easily be extrapolated to lower levels of detail.
- **Labile:** The architecture is flexible enough to allow changes in business needs as digital transformation and the biz-tech ecosystem evolve.

25) The additional components of the REAL, logical architecture that surround the information pillars (PMD, MGD, and HSI) and information preparation functions (instantiation, assimilation, and reification) are:
- Utilization
- Organization
- Choreography.

26) Data managers may mistakenly assume a unidirectional flow of information from the information pillars to the utilization tools. Many people activities feed information back "down" into the information space, most obviously through analytical and planning activities. People in the business can and do generate messages that feed into the environment as a result of insights gained at the utilization level. Data managers must pay particular attention to both of these "reverse" information flows and their impact on data governance.

27) Insurance data managers need to understand the difference between emerging architectures and architectural patterns, i.e., diagrams drawn by vendors. They should understand the pros and cons of each when proposed as solutions to digital business needs.

28) In traditional architectural approaches, functions are often arranged in layers with well-defined, bounded purposes, and access or data flows up or down the layers in a controlled manner. DISA adopts a somewhat uncommon, pillared approach.

29) Issues with most data warehouse architecture approaches include:
- Lack of agility to respond to changes in business-driven data needs.
- Delays in delivery due to delays in every layer.

30) The concerns that influence decisions on where data is stored: on premises, in the Cloud, or in some hybrid configuration, include:
- Financial considerations and preferences, in particular, choosing between operational and capital expenditure (Opex vs. Capex).
- Existing investments in hardware, software, skills, and openness to change.
- Maturity and ongoing viability of existing business models and IT solutions.
- Relative strengths and directions of different products in their Cloud or on-premises features.

31) The important characteristics of an enterprise data model (EDM) for ensuring consistency across different data and information stores are:
- As a common data model, it is vital that its structure is primarily top-down, defining and agreeing on information categories, data classes, or subject areas that anchor all lower levels.
- For each subject area, a high-level data model defining entities, attributes, and relationships or similar concepts is agreed across the major business areas.
- Applying these high-level models to the pillars creates a framework that is consistent across the different technical implementations and locations and lays the foundation for shared CSI.
- When a pillar resides outside the enterprise, the model is used to drive a mapping between external data and the preferred internal data.
- The EDM also serves as the basis for mapping data inputs to outputs during instantiation, assimilation, and reification.

Data Warehouse—Data Management Tradition and Foundation

Educational Objectives

Upon completion of this assignment, you should be able to:

1. Describe the layered data warehouse approach and list its strengths and weaknesses.
2. Describe the dimensional data warehouse approach and list its strengths and weaknesses.
3. Describe the role and importance of data modeling in data warehousing.
4. Explore current approaches to address data warehousing strengths and weaknesses.
5. Position the data warehouse in the DISA.
6. Describe the relationship of data warehousing to data management.

For each assignment, define or describe each of the Key Terms and Concepts and answer each of the Review and Discussion Questions.

Key Terms and Concepts

Business Data Warehouse:

Business Data Directory:

Operational Systems:

Informational Systems:

Data Warehouse:

Dependent Data Marts:

Independent Data Marts:

Online Analytical Processing (OLAP):

Multidimensional Analytics:

Review Questions

1) Define the business data warehouse (EBIS) as presented in the IBM Systems Journal.

2) Identify the three areas that need clarification regarding the IBM data warehouse.

3) Explain why direct access to operational systems was not an acceptable solution to the need for information to manage the business.

4) Identify the data management role associated with feeding informational systems from operational systems.

5) Identify the business issue with feeding informational systems from operational systems.

6) List and identify the data characteristics of the Inmon data warehouse.

7) A successful data warehouse requires the balancing of two views of the subject-oriented characteristic of the Inmon data warehouse. Identify the two views.

8) List the fundamental principles of data warehouse architecture.

9) One of the principles of the data warehouse is that it provides a single data/information source for business decision-making. How does this relate in the language of the DISA at the logical, REAL level?

10) How is data/information with a consistent business and technical context derived for the data warehouse?

11) Identify the issue that led to the development of the layered data warehouse.

12) The layered data warehouse resolved the competing objectives of warehouse design. How was the practical application more complicated?

13) Why does the layered data warehouse model show unidirectional flows of data from sources to the enterprise data warehouse to data marts, and why is this misleading?

14) What is the data management issue related to independent data marts and when might they be considered?

15) Describe the relationship between the enterprise data model (EDM) and the layered data warehouse.

16) Identify the levels of the enterprise data model for the layered data warehouse, which is presented as a pyramid.

17) Identify the chief strength and weakness of the layered data warehouse.

18) Which of the following is NOT a strength of the layered data warehouse?
   A. Reconciliation of data from disparate sources, eliminating inconsistencies in semantics and timing between them.
   B. Creation of a common, consistent, and integrated historical record or "memory" of the business, especially where such data is not preserved in the operational sources.
   C. Development and delivery are more complex, requiring a politically acceptable staged approach and coordination of deliverables and timing across all business departments and IT.
   D. Provision of a common, consistent, and integrated base of data for informational systems and decision-making support.

19) Which of the following is NOT a weakness of the layered data warehouse?
   A. In operation, data must pass through and be stored in multiple layers (including hidden staging layers), delaying its arrival to the business when needed, which may impact near-real-time decision-making processes such as operational BI.
   B. Establishment of a shared, common context language around core business information and its meaning, allowing the relationship between divergent usage across functions and departments to be bridged.
   C. Modifications and upgrades to the system to address new or changed business needs may be time-consuming and error-prone due to the number and complexity of layers and feeds.
   D. Upfront creation, acquisition, and customization of an enterprise data model are required, which can be time-consuming and/or expensive.

20) Describe the dimensional modeling approach that underlies the dimensional data warehouse.

21) The origins of the approach underlying the dimensional data warehouse focused on a data structure with what two characteristics?

22) How do OLAP tools facilitate analyses needed by businesspeople?

23) Describe an OLAP cube and how it is used in analyses.

24) The approach to the development of a dimensional data warehouse differs from that of a layered warehouse. Describe the differences.

25) Which of the following is NOT a strength of the dimensional data warehouse?
   A.   Early delivery of business value through data mart-like subsets of data is possible without the need for upfront EDM and EDW development.
   B.   Speedy and efficient development in natural stages related to business processes of the complete data warehouse is supported.
   C.   A single ETL layer is not needed for data delivery to the business, which can be more timely.
   D.   None of the above.

26) Which of the following is a weakness of the dimensional data warehouse?
   A. Absence of a formal EDM makes it more challenging to confirm consistency of data naming, relationships, etc., and offers less support for data management and governance.
   B. It is not well suited to near-real-time use due to the rapid growth in data volumes.
   C. The dimension construct poses challenges with temporal data, updates, and late-arriving data.
   D. None of the above.

27) What types of organizations would favor a dimensional data warehouse?

28) Describe a hybrid approach to a data warehouse that would be attractive to more complex organizations. What are the benefits and disadvantages of this approach?

29) The data vault is the most common form of ensemble data models. Describe the concept of a data vault and identify its benefits.

30) A data vault is generally constructed in two layers. Identify these layers.

31) Identify some of the considerations associated with moving the data warehouse towards real-time analytics.

32) What approaches can be used to solve some of the problems associated with moving to real-time analytics?

33) Where is the data warehouse placed within the digital information systems architecture (DISA) and how does it differ from the ideal represented by the DISA?

34) How does the digital information systems architecture (DISA) offer a way to reduce the conflict between the need for improved timeliness with the need for a high level of consistency in the data warehouse?

35) Describe the idealized PMD, the current state overlaying a data warehouse and the future possibilities.

36) Describe how the emergence of the data warehouse approach expanded the interest in data management.

37) How does data governance support data warehouse initiatives?

38) Identify the roles for data managers in developing and expanding the data warehouse.

39) How does implementing an enterprise-wide data warehouse provide the impetus and business case for a data management initiative?

Discussion Questions

NOTE: The questions below are intended to continue to challenge you to test your knowledge of the required reading by applying what you have studied to real-life situations.

No suggested answers are provided at the end of the assignment for these types of open discussion questions. Answers may vary by student and will depend on their organization's culture, resources, and processes.

1) Discuss which types of data warehouse, layered, dimensional, or hybrid, exist in your organization or would be best suited for your company.

2) Discuss what the data management challenges have been or would be in developing a warehouse in your organization. Who would champion the effort? Who would be more critical or cautious about it?

Answers to Assignment 4 Questions

NOTE: These answers are provided to give students a basic understanding of acceptable types of responses. They are often not the only valid answers and are not intended to provide an exhaustive response to the questions.

Key Terms and Concepts

Business Data Warehouse: A repository containing public and personal data at raw, detailed, and summary levels from operational and local (personal) systems.

Business Data Directory: Description of data in the business data warehouse sourced from a data dictionary and business process definitions.

Operational Systems: Systems that run the business, in areas such as underwriting and claims, and contain and manage real-time data, optimized for read/write use.

Informational Systems: Includes today's data warehouses and business intelligence (BI) tools. Used to manage the business and are read-only in design.

Data Warehouse: A subject-oriented, nonvolatile, integrated, time-variant collection of data in support of management decisions.

Dependent Data Marts: Data marts sourced directly from the enterprise data warehouse.

Independent Data Marts: Data marts sourced directly from the operational environment.

Online Analytical Processing (OLAP): Processing made up of numerous, speculative "what-if" and/or "why" data model scenarios executed within the context of some specific historical basis and perspective.

Multidimensional Analytics: Allow data to be examined along multiple axes simultaneously.

Review Questions

1) The business data warehouse is the single logical storehouse of all the information used to report on the business, presented as a set of tables in a relational database environment. Data may physically reside in multiple locations, but the end user sees only a single source that satisfies all informational needs.

2) The three areas that need clarification regarding the IBM data warehouse are:
   - While the description includes a relational database environment as the foundation of the warehouse, the concern is with the relational model rather than the technology.

- Presenting users with multiple views of the data of interest has been challenging due to performance issues with multi-joins in relational databases. The result has been the development of data marts to provide the needed views, which are fed by enterprise data warehouses.
- While business needs drove the idea of a single logical repository for a consistent, reconciled view of data from multiple sources, limitations in database technology led to a single physical database. Advances in technology have made logical warehouses more practical in recent years.

3) Operational systems were entirely mainframe based and carefully designed to accelerate processing and minimize storage requirements. Through arcane coding and ingenious programming, they often made the data therein almost indecipherable to businesspeople. Furthermore, IT departments were understandably reluctant to allow direct access to operational data, lest it impact daily operations, given the long-running and/or complex calculations required to summarize and analyze transactional data.

4) Data from disparate systems and departments is likely to be defined differently depending on its original use. Making such data widely available requires reconciling its content and refactoring its definitions to enable consistent use by the business, needs that the evolving data management discipline was central to articulating.

5) With multiple data pathways feeding diverse DSS tools on different platforms used by different departments, the opportunities for confusion multiply rapidly. Decision makers receive different reports about the state of the business, depending on the bearer of the news. Departmental heads and, especially, the head of IT are dispatched to resolve the apparent discrepancies, wasting time and resources on problems that should never have arisen if a well-governed, centrally driven environment was in place.

6) The data characteristics of the Inmon data warehouse are:
- **Subject-oriented**: Data should be represented in terms and structures that are familiar to businesspeople.
- **Integrated**: Differences in data from disparate systems should be reconciled in various ways to deliver a "single version of the truth (SVOT) that can be used across the enterprise.
- **Nonvolatile**: Users should be able to recreate a business situation as of a particular date and time in the past, either for reporting or as a basis for what-if simulations.
- **Time-variant**: All records in the warehouse are time-stamped.

7) Inmon's subject-oriented view is designed to directly support decision makers, while an enterprise data model view, as described by Sowa and Zachman, is aimed at integrating data from diverse sources.

8) The fundamental principles of data warehouse architecture include:
- A single data/information source for business decision-making support.
- Widespread and distributed information availability.
- Information in a consistent business (and technical) context.
- Automated information/data delivery.
- Information quality and ownership in the data warehouse.

9) Data in the warehouse comes from multiple, mostly internal, largely operational sources and is part of process-mediated data. This data must be cleansed and reconciled through the REAL function of

assimilation before it is made available to business people, and thus becomes the single ultimate source for formal, legally binding information-informed management.

10) Business experts provide data definitions that are included in data catalogs. Data modeling helps describe relationships between different sources of information, discover synonyms and homonyms, and identify conflicting definitions. These activities provide a foundation for populating the data warehouse in a consistent manner.

11) The twin objectives of reconciling data from multiple, disparate sources and providing easily understood subsets/views of that data to businesspeople were simultaneously unachievable in the relational databases of the time.

12) In practice, additional hidden layers or staging areas were often required to prepare data for the EDW or data marts.

13) The design emphasizes data management principles and ensures data consistency in the upper layers. It was, in effect, an over-simplification of the real business needs which demand that data and information, such as planning forecasts created in informational systems, are subsequently made available in the operational environment.

14) From a data management perspective, this is a return to spaghetti development. Independent data marts can be valuable as a stopgap in early data warehouse rollouts where there is no other way to satisfy an urgent business need.

15) The EDM spans the entire spectrum of data creation and use in the business:
   - Provides the structure and context for the EDW as well as for the subsets of data in the data marts.
   - Is the basis for all the ETL logic between all layers in the architecture, in conjunction with other application-level models where appropriate.
   - Is the foundation for all understanding and discussion of the context of data and its relationship to the information used by businesspeople.

16) The levels of the enterprise data model for the layered data warehouse, presented as a pyramid, are:
   - Business concepts and classes, consisting of perhaps a dozen of the highest-level entities or subject areas of interest to the business, and their breakdown into different classes or categories, form the apex of the pyramid.
   - An enterprise data model, which identifies and describes in detail all entities, attributes, and relationships used throughout the business, typically presented as an entity-relationship diagram, is the next level of the pyramid.
   - The third level of the pyramid is a logical application model that includes specialized models for the EDW, data marts, and operational systems.
   - Physical data designs that apply physical implementation constraints to the EDW, data marts, and operational systems form the base level of the pyramid.

17) The chief strength of the layered data warehouse is its focus on providing well-managed, consistent, high-quality data to decision makers and other businesspeople. This strength leads to its chief weakness: a lack of agility in both development and data delivery.

18) The correct answer choice is C. This is a weakness, not a strength, of a layered data warehouse.

19) The correct answer choice is B. This is actually a strength, not a weakness, of a layered data warehouse.

20) The dimensional modeling approach uses a single-layer structure, with no concept of an enterprise data warehouse or data marts.

21) The origins of the approach underlying the dimensional data warehouse focused on a data structure with the following characteristics:
- Easily understood by businesspeople.
- Optimized for the speedy return of results to a relatively flexible set of user queries.

22) OLAP tools enable users to analyze multidimensional data interactively from multiple perspectives.

23) Data in a cube (or hypercube) is composed of multiple, hierarchical dimensions. Each location within the cube represents a fact and a quantity or measure of interest. Within the cube, analysts can roll up or drill down to view data along the dimensional hierarchies and examine measures at different levels of detail. Slicing allows the analyst to focus on a specific perspective or slice of the cube, while dicing effectively rotates the cube.

24) The dimensional warehouse is built from a process viewpoint rather than around subject areas defined in the EDM, which is the basis for a layered warehouse. This process viewpoint enables the development of "first-level" data marts to support a single department or business function from a single operational source. A full data warehouse can be built incrementally by extending the range of processes covered and operational sources included. Analytic consistency in the dimensional data warehouse is ensured and future development costs are reduced. This differs from the layered warehouse, where all sources and functions are modeled in the EDW and built into the warehouse at the onset.

25) The correct answer choice is C.

26) The correct answer choice is D.

27) The following types of organizations would favor a dimensional data warehouse:
- Organizations where most BI activity is based on multidimensional analytics.
- Smaller organizations may find that the delivery of a dimensional warehouse is smoother and less costly.

28) In larger, more complex organizations, dimensional data marts may be fed from a centrally managed and delivered EDW. This offers the data management benefits accruing from an EDM and enables a focus on cross-enterprise data consistency through the design and development of the EDW. However, such a hybrid approach has the disadvantages of higher technical and organizational complexity.

29) The data vault model is a detail-oriented, historical-tracking, and specially linked set of normalized tables that support one or more functional business areas. This design offers a flexible, scalable, consistent, and adaptable way to address enterprise-wide needs.

30) The two layers of a data vault are:
- The raw or operational data vault contains raw, unmodified historical data, integrated by business key to ensure full auditability back to the source data.

- The business data vault takes the raw data and manipulates it according to business rules to transform it into useful information.

31) Considerations associated with moving the data warehouse towards real-time analytics include:
- There exists a fundamental physical limit to how far consistency and timeliness can be balanced in a distributed environment.
- Legacy mainframe operational systems likely hamper efforts to deliver data more promptly.

32) Approaches that can be used to solve some of the problems associated with moving to real-time analytics include:
- New technologies may offer some solutions.
- Expectation-setting discussions about the business need for real-time data limiting it to areas where cross-functional consistency is less important.

33) The data warehouse is a component of process-mediated data (PMD), one of the pillars of the logical information architecture. However, the data warehouse contains both operational and informational data, which are not separated in the idealized DISA.

34) DISA offers a path to reduce the conflict: integrating and consolidating operational and informational systems and data enabled by advances in hardware and software technology.

35) The idealized PMD, the current state overlaying a data warehouse, and the future possibilities can be described:
- In the DISA, operational systems (instantiation) create transactions, which, through the process of assimilation, are derived and reconciled in the upper part of the PMD. The PMD box can be thought of as residing in a "single" environment: technologically consistent and likely distributed over multiple machines.
- In the current environment, operational systems residing across multiple, diverse environments encapsulate their transactional data entry and storage systems. ETL tools extract this data, transform it, and load it into the data warehouse and data marts in a physically separate system or systems. The "PMD" box is a logical construct that includes these multiple physical stores.
- In the near future, as hardware and software evolve to allow handling of both read/write operational work and read-only analytical work, a combined operational/informational system, containing transactional data as well as reconciled and derived data, can be added to create a physically instantiated PMD similar to the PMD in the DISA.

36) The emergence of the data warehouse approach expanded the interest in data management in the following ways:
- The aggregation of data and provision of information to executive management revealed inconsistencies in understanding and in the measurement of business importance across departments, leading to poor decisions and/or costly efforts to "correct" the figures.
- Efforts to create reconciled data warehouse artifacts are regularly hindered by a lack of clear definitions of what the data means, where it came from, its quality and accuracy, and how it is used.

37) Data governance supports data warehouse initiatives in the following ways:
- Data governance ensures the existence and availability of high-quality data throughout the organization and across the complete lifecycle of the data.
- Data governance also ensures that data controls are implemented that support business objectives.

- Data governance processes offer data warehouse implementers the organizational framework required to create and maintain a first-rate, enterprise-wide information asset.

38) The data management team should be intimately involved and play a key role in defining governance processes that ensure ongoing data quality, whether the organization is developing an initial warehouse, redesigning an existing one, or expanding the data marts to meet emerging business needs.

39) Data integration artifacts, including the enterprise and logical application models, ETL designs, and data mart requirements, may provide the initial roadmap and exposition of data use, both good and bad, across the organization.

From Big Data to Data Lakes and Beyond

Educational Objectives

Upon completion of this assignment, you should be able to:

1. Define big data, its business uses, and its challenges.
2. Relate big data to human-sourced information and machine-generated data.
3. Describe the concept of a data lake, its history, and its architectural positioning.
4. List the strengths and weaknesses of the data lake approach.
5. Position the data lake in the Digital Information Systems Architecture (DISA).
6. Explore current approaches to address combined data warehouse/data lake environments, including the logical data warehouse, data fabric, data lakehouse, and data mesh.
7. Describe how the data lake impacts data management and data quality.

For each assignment, define or describe each of the Key Terms and Concepts and answer each of the Review and Discussion Questions.

Key Terms and Concepts

Big Data:

Human-Sourced Information:

Machine-Generated:

Clickstream Data:

Data Lake:

Schema-O-Write:

Schema-On-Read:

Logical Data Warehouse:

Data Virtualization:

Data Lakehouse:

Data Fabric:

Active Metadata:

Domain-Driven Design:

Data Mesh:

Review Questions

1) Identify the progression of storage sizes from kilobyte to zettabyte.

2) What is the estimate of process-mediated data as a percentage of all data processed for business purposes, and how does this relate to the volume of data in the datasphere?

3) Although the volumes of data generated are staggering, what is the good news for data managers? What is the bad news?

4) Given all this data, what is the challenge for business and data managers?

5) What are the problems with Wikipedia and subsequent definitions of big data?

6) Describe human-sourced information (HSI).

7) How does HSI bring value to business? How does business use human-sourced information?

8) What is the value of clickstream data to business?

9) Characterize machine-generated data (MGD) produced by the Internet of Things (IOT).

10) Data managers consider the characteristics of human-sourced information to determine how to store, manage, and ensure it is of sufficient quality to serve its intended purposes. Identify those characteristics.

11) Data managers consider the characteristics of machine-generated data to determine how to store, manage, and ensure it is of sufficient quality to serve its intended purposes. Identify those characteristics.

12) Data managers also divide the world of data/information into categories for purposes of understanding aspects of its creation, use, storage, etc. List and describe these categories.

13) What is the conclusion that can be drawn about data lakes from the Capgemini design?

14) What is the data management perspective on data lakes, and what has been the response to data management's concerns?

15) What is the business benefit of data lakes?

16) What are some of the questions and concerns that need to be asked about the data to be stored in a data lake?

17) What has been the most serious criticism of data lakes?

18) What are the challenges data lakes pose to data managers in comparison to data warehouses?

19) Position the data lake and data warehouse in the digital information systems architecture (DISA).

20) In what ways does data from the data lake support the business's goals?

21) What roles do instantiation, assimilation, and reification play with respect to the data lake in the DISA?

22) Why must data warehouses and data lakes coexist, and what are the concerns for managing them?

23) How does an organization determine the relationship between the data warehouse and data lake?

24) One scenario of how to position an existing on-premises warehouse and data lake involves moving both to the cloud. What are the takeaways from this example?

25) Describe a simplified view of how a data warehouse, operational systems, and data lake might coexist without focusing on storage location or platform.

26) Describe the concept of a data lakehouse.

27) Describe the fundamental premise of the lakehouse and its benefits.

28) True or False? Data Fabric is a technological platform whose sole objective is to combine various types of data storage, access, preparation, analytics, and security tools in a fully compliant manner.

29) True or False? Domain-Driven Design is the concept that the structure and language of software should match the "business domain" in which it operates and underlies the data mesh architectural pattern.

30) What are the benefits of a logical data warehouse as a conceptual architecture for a combined data warehouse/data lake environment?

31) The lack of metadata for the data lake raises a number of issues. What recent development has improved data quality in the lake?

32) What feature of data in the data lake will help limit the impact of quality issues as compared to data in the warehouse?

33) Given that the expectation of quality is lower for data in the lake than in the warehouse, what is the likely focus for data managers?

Discussion Questions

NOTE: The questions below are intended to continue to challenge you to test your knowledge of the required reading by applying what you have studied to real-life situations.

No suggested answers are provided at the end of the assignment for these types of open discussion questions. Answers may vary by student and will depend on their organization's culture, resources, and processes.

1) For your organization, what would be the biggest data management issues related to a data lake, and how might you go about resolving them?

2) What type of external data do you think might be valuable to link to your organization's internal data? What context-setting information would you like to have? What "health warnings" would you attach to it?

Answers to Assignment 5 Questions

NOTE: These answers are provided to give students a basic understanding of acceptable types of responses. They are often not the only valid answers and are not intended to provide an exhaustive response to the questions.

Key Terms and Concepts

Big Data: Per Wikipedia, Big data usually includes data sets with sizes beyond the ability of commonly used software tools to capture, curate, manage, and process data within a tolerable elapsed time. Big data philosophy encompasses unstructured, semi-structured, and structured data; however, the main focus is on unstructured data. Big data 'size' is a constantly moving target, ranging from a few dozen terabytes to many zettabytes as of 2012.

Human-Sourced Information: The subjective and highly personal record of people's beliefs and declarations about and recollections of what has happened, or may happen, in the physical world, including their relationships to and within their environment.

Machine-Generated Data: Consists of events or measures gathered by electronic devices at known times.

Clickstream Data: A detailed log generated by a web server of how users navigate through a website or series of websites and typically includes events and measures such as the pages visited, time spent on each page, how they arrived on the page, and where they went next.

Data Lake: A landing zone for externally sourced big data in its most raw, unvarnished form, consisting of as many stores and types of storage as needed, allowing users such as analysts and data scientists to "play" with the data and extract insights from it.

Schema-O-Write: In traditional data warehousing, the schema (or structure or model) of a relational database must be defined in advance, and incoming data must be aligned with it when it is written or loaded.

Schema-On-Read: In a data lake, data is loaded as-is, leaving the application of any desired schema to the user of that data when it is read from the store.

Logical Data Warehouse: The architectural pattern showcases the ability to access data in multiple forms and locations through a single access point.

Data Virtualization: The ability to access data in multiple forms and locations through a single access point.

Data Lakehouse: An architectural pattern that proposes that a combination of the best qualities of a data warehouse and data lake can be achieved by a new system design implementing similar data structures and data management features to those in a warehouse, directly on a kind of low-cost storage used for data lakes and running in the cloud.

Data Fabric: A distributed data management platform, where the sole objective is to combine various types of data storage, access, preparation, analytics, and security tools in a fully compliant manner so that data management tasks become easy and smooth.

Active Metadata: Metadata that can change and grow automatically in real time as the environment evolves.

Domain-Driven Design: The concept that structure and language of software should match the business domain in which it operates.

Data Mesh: An alternative to the centralized paradigm of the data warehouse or lake, a data architecture where business units are responsible for the data they need, from initial creation to consumption. Data is delivered by the business unit, complete with metadata and code needed to manage and use it.

Review Questions

1. The progression of storage sizes from kilobyte to zettabyte is:
    - Kilobyte (KB)   = 103 bytes
    - Megabyte (MB)   = 106 bytes
    - Gigabyte (GB)   = 109 bytes
    - Terabyte(TB)   = 1012 bytes
    - Petabyte (PB)   =1015 bytes
    - Exabyte (EB)   = 1015 bytes
    - Zettabyte (ZB)   = 1018 bytes

2. Traditional data, process-mediated data (PMD), accounts for perhaps 1% of the data processed by enterprises for business purposes, which is about 10% of the total global datasphere.

3. The good news for data managers is that 90% of the data in the datasphere is of little to no importance to the business community, consisting mainly of videos and social media content. The bad news is that the remaining 5-10% still represents significant data volumes, both in real terms and compared to the traditional PMD data volumes that enterprise IT has been used to managing and governing in existing operational and informational environments.

4. For business, the challenge is making sense of all this data and, more importantly, extracting actionable information from it. Data managers must decide how far the quality of big data can be realistically managed, the cost of doing so, and the impacts on PMD quality management in circumstances of fixed or shrinking IT budgets.

5. According to these definitions, big data is both poorly defined and refers to a wide variety of things. In the Wikipedia definition, the terms are vague. In the later definition by Laney and others, the terms used, e.g., volume, velocity, variety, etc., represent continuous variables.

6. Human-sourced information is loosely structured, textual, and multiplex (image/video/audio), spanning the full spectrum of timeliness/consistency, from in-flight messages to historical documents and everything in between.

7. HSI provides fundamental insights into the inner, personal landscape of people's minds and their relationships. Its collection and analysis are thus driven mainly by sales and marketing functions wishing to understand prospects' and customers' judgments and intentions, as well as to predict or influence future behaviors. Legal departments and insurance policy writers also produce and consume large quantities of HSI, even if its composition into final documents is increasingly automated. Claims departments also rely extensively on HSI.

8. Business can garner deep insights into customer and prospect behavior and intentions by combining clickstream data combined with HSI.

9. MGD from the IOT arrives in organizations in vast quantities from external sources over which the receiver has little or no control. The structure or content of such data may be poorly understood or may vary over time. The data itself may be incomplete or in error. Different or upgraded devices may produce new or different measures and events.

10. Data managers consider the following characteristics of human-sourced information to determine how to store, manage, and ensure it is of sufficient quality to serve its intended purposes:
    - Loosely structured, often large chunks/records.
    - Human speeds.
    - Volume outdoes velocity.
    - Embedded context.
    - Fluid and culturally determined semantics.
    - Can be modeled only when received.
    - Describes sentiment: may indicate likely behaviors.
    - Text mining, video, image, and voice recognition.
    - Informational, unidirectional.

11. Data managers consider the following characteristics of machine-generated data to determine how to store, manage, and ensure it is of sufficient quality to serve its intended purposes:
    - Semi-structured, mostly tiny chunks/ records.
    - Machine speeds.
    - Velocity outdoes volume.
    - Separately documented context.
    - Engineered and changing, versioned semantics.
    - Modeled in advance but may change without notice.
    - Records states and actions: predicts future states and actions.
    - Data mining, time series, and streaming analytics.
    - Operational, bi-directional.

12. Data managers also divide the world of data/information into the following categories for purposes of understanding aspects of its creation, use, storage, etc.:
    - **Entertainment**: Image and video content created or consumed for entertainment purposes.
    - **Non-entertainment image/video**: Image and video content for non-entertainment purposes, such as video surveillance footage or advertising.
    - **Productivity data**: Traditional productivity-driven data such as files on PCs and servers, log files, and metadata.
    - **Embedded**: Data created by embedded devices, machine-to-machine, and IoT.

13. The conclusion is that a data lake is a "container" for a variety of different types of data storage and access technologies with no necessary coordination or alignment of the data residing there. Data is

thus stored in flat files (HDFS), relational databases (SQL), and non-relational databases/stores (NoSQL) at the discretion of those loading or requesting it.

14. From a data management perspective, the data lake approach was untenable in the medium- to long-term for any organization pursuing data governance goals. More recent data lake designs include mechanisms for managing externally sourced data, reflecting the understanding that externally sourced data cannot stand alone in analytics and must be combined with other internally sourced data to deliver meaningful insights.

15. Data lakes provide access to externally sourced data in raw form, allowing analysts and data scientists to explore and extract insights.

16. The questions and concerns that need to be asked about the data to be stored in a data lake include:
    - Should we store everything? The costs of hardware, software, and skilled data management can be prohibitive.
    - Is all data of equal value? Who determines the value and priorities of the data to be collected?
    - If IT builds it, will the business find it useful? The effort to develop a data lake can't be technology driven. Business must be involved.
    - Are quality and consistency no longer needed? How should quality and consistency be guaranteed when external data is combined with strictly governed internal data?
    - What problem are we trying to solve? The overall data lake process carries the risk of delivering piecemeal solutions to specific needs without an overarching direction.

17. Since the data lake accepts any data without oversight or governance, users can't assess data quality or the lineage of findings from other data analysts. And without metadata, every subsequent use of the data means analysts have to start from scratch.

18. The challenges data lakes pose to data managers in comparison to data warehouses include:
    - Data scientists who prefer unfettered access to data may resist data management quality and governance practices.
    - Data quality issues associated with data from poorly regulated or defined external sources are more complex than those from data warehouse implementations.

19. The data warehouse, built of reconciled transactional data, resides in the process-mediated data (PMD) pillar of the DISA. The data lake, composed of human-sourced information (HSI) and machine-generated data (MGD), is built across the HSI and MGD pillars of the DISA. However, the data lake does not completely occupy these pillars; other HSI and MGD may exist outside the data lake.

20. Some analytic models are used to inform tactical and strategic decisions; others must be "productionalized" to drive operational behavior and decisions and fed back into the systems that produced the data in the first place.

21. The data lake is sourced from human-sourced data and machine-generated data through instantiation. In subsequent processing, assimilation cleanses the lake data and links it to data in other stores. Reification provides integrated access to the disparate data stores, including those in the data lake, for businesspeople, analysts, and data scientists.

22. Each serves a distinct business need. The warehouse emphasizes data consistency, while the data lake favors timeliness. Understanding their relationship and relative positioning, specifically with

respect to logical data flows and linkages between them, is vital for appropriate data management in the combined environment.

23. There is no one-size-fits-all solution. The relationship between a data warehouse and a data lake is ultimately specific to the organization in question and its existing IT environment, in terms of both technology and physical/geographical implementation.

24. The takeaways from this example include:
    - Moving an on-premises data lake to the cloud may take advantage of the cloud elasticity and the opportunity to incur operational rather than capital expenses.
    - Costs to move the data warehouse will depend on the warehouse product used and the method of migration.
    - If the operational systems that feed the warehouse are on-premises, ongoing transfer costs may be prohibitive.

25. On one side, the operational system feeds transactions to the warehouse. Across from the warehouse, the lake is fed from external or transient internal data. CSI supports all three systems. Some warehouse data may be copied into the lake and models from the lake feed back into the operational systems. Sitting over the warehouse and lake is a data virtualization layer for reporting/business intelligence, analytics/AI.

26. A data lakehouse is an architectural pattern that combines the best features of a data warehouse and a data lake. This design implements data structures and data management features similar to those of a data warehouse, using low-cost storage for data lakes and running in the cloud. The concept hasn't gained much traction since there is limited detail about how to achieve the vision.

27. The fundamental premise of the lakehouse is that both warehouse and lake data are stored in the same object store, whether highly structured relational data or a more loosely structured format. This approach eliminates much of the traditional copying of data from the lake to the warehouse and is particularly powerful when the majority of operational data originates in the cloud.

28. The statement is False. Data Fabric is a data management platform.

29. The statement is True.

30. The following are the benefits of a logical data warehouse as a conceptual architecture for a combined data warehouse/data lake environment:
    - Data virtualization offers a fast and effective approach to integrating existing lake and warehouse environments.
    - Offers early business value.
    - Allows and drives data management advances, particularly as a result of its enterprise data model foundation, which requires significant and documented knowledge of data resources, meanings, and even ownership/stewardship of the content of the data lake.

31. While the lack of metadata for the data lake raises a number of issues, the emergence of data catalogs has helped significantly improved the quality of data in the lake.

32. The data lake is primarily designed for big data, whether externally or internally sourced, often with a short shelf life and thus with lower expectations for overall quality than for process-mediated data that reflects the legally binding history of the business.

33. Data managers will likely define and document the circumstances under which and how lake and warehouse data can be used safely together, and the "health warnings" that should be attached to such combined data, as well as to the contents of the data lake itself.

Databases and Stores

Educational Objectives

Upon completion of this assignment, you should be able to:

1. List and define the broad categories of data storage and management tools.
2. Describe their evolution.
3. Define the relational model and explain what a relational database does.
4. Describe the different types of relational databases and where they are used.
5. Define the meaning of Hadoop and NoSQL.
6. Explain the purpose of HDFS and other key Hadoop components.
7. Describe the different types of NoSQL data stores and their varied uses.
8. Describe the high-level implications of cloud and hybrid data storage implementations and products.

For each assignment, define or describe each of the Key Terms and Concepts and answer each of the Review and Discussion Questions.

Key Terms and Concepts

Sequential (or Flat) File:

Direct Access (or Random Access) Files:

MapReduce:

Object Store:

Hadoop:

Structured Query Language (SQL):

NoSQL:

Relational Model:

Relational Database:

Database Normalization:

Symmetric Multiprocessing (SMP):

Massively Parallel Processing (MPP):

Review Questions

1) Describe the characteristics of sequential or flat files.

2) Describe the processing problems related to sequential files.

3) Describe characteristics of direct access or random access files.

4) Identify the capabilities typical of object stores.

5) Identify the focus of object stores.

6) What conditions drove the popularization of the Hadoop Distributed File System (HDFS)?

7) What was the focus of the first class of database management systems (DBMS)?

8) Identify some of the issues related to early database management systems.

9) Describe the major developments of the relational model and relational databases.

10) Describe the relational model underpinnings of a relational database.

11) How do real-world relational databases differ from the theoretical relational model?

12) List the three basic concepts that are fundamental to all relational database design.

13) Identify the types of problems that can be resolved by normalization.

14) When is third normal form (3NF) most effective? When is it less effective?

15) Describe the ACID model.

16) Identify the problems associated with transaction-oriented databases.

17) Where were transactional relational databases most effective? Least effective?

18) For which type of data (machine-generated data, process-mediated data, or human-sourced information) are relational databases suitable?

19) What conditions lead to the development of analytical appliances or data warehouse appliances?

20) Why can analytical appliances be thought of as large data marts?

21) What benefits does solid-state disk storage (SSD) offer?

22) What is columnar storage and what value does it bring to the processing?

23) What are the advantages and disadvantages of analytical appliances?

24) Identify two recent trends in analytic appliances.

25) What is persistent memory and what value does it provide?

26) What is the downside of the HDFS system design and what approach is taken to mitigate this issue?

27) What is the suitability of HDFS for process-mediated data and human-sourced information?

28) List the characteristics that may be included in a NoSQL database management system.

29) What does it mean for a database management system to be BASE?

30) Identify the different NoSQL data stores described in the text.

31) Where are wide column stores most effective?

32) Describe a document store.

33) What is the concern that databases need to balance, and what is the criticism of NoSQL in this regard?

34) Describe the two types of graph databases.

35) What is an object store and how does it compare to HDFS?

36) What is the challenge of these distributed databases and environments?

Discussion Questions

NOTE: The questions below are intended to continue to challenge you to test your knowledge of the required reading by applying what you have studied to real-life situations.

No suggested answers are provided at the end of the assignment for these types of open discussion questions. Answers may vary by student and will depend on their organization's culture, resources, and processes.

1) What types of data storage are in use in your company? How have storage types changed over time, and how has this change benefited the user community?

2) Has your company begun to move to cloud storage? What has that process looked like?

Answers to Assignment 6 Questions

NOTE: These answers are provided to give students a basic understanding of acceptable types of responses. They are often not the only valid answers and are not intended to provide an exhaustive response to the questions.

Key Terms and Concepts

Sequential (or Flat) File: A file that consists of an ordered string of characters (bytes) that are read one by one and in order, from start to finish. New data can only be written at the end.

Direct Access (or Random Access) Files: Files that offer a variety of ways of directly jumping to a record of interest, allowing access in roughly the same timescale to any record in the file, no matter how large.

MapReduce: A Google product providing a programming framework and implementation that was ideal for processing large data sets.

Object Store: Storage concept where each object typically includes the data of interest, relevant metadata, and a globally unique identifier.

Hadoop: A complex, extended, and deeply interdependent but independently developed ecosystem of mostly open source software to collect, prepare, process, and deliver data for analytical purposes. The extended Hadoop system can include flat files, relational databases, and NoSQL data storage.

Structured Query Language (SQL): The most used access method to relational databases; it can be and is used to access other data structures.

NoSQL: Refers to databases or data stores (rather than access languages) that do not adhere to the relational paradigm.

Relational Model: (Wikipedia) An approach to managing data using a structure and language consistent with first-order predicate logic ... where all data is represented in terms of tuples [sequences or ordered lists of elements], grouped into relations.

Relational Database: A database organized by relations.

Database Normalization: The process of determining how much redundancy exists in a table and eliminating it to the most appropriate extent to optimize database consistency, performance, and size.

Symmetric Multiprocessing (SMP): A first form of parallel processing where multiple processors share memory and other resources under a single copy of the operating system.

Massively Parallel Processing (MPP): Parallel processing where each processor has full control of separate memory and other resources.

Review Questions

1) Characteristics of sequential or flat files include:
   - Sequential files consist of an ordered string of characters (bytes) that are read one by one.
   - New data can only be written to the end of the file.
   - Generally, bytes are grouped into words or fields, organized into records that contain information about a single object of interest.
   - Fields can be fixed or variable length.
   - Key-value pairs are common, where the first field or group of fields identifies the item of interest (i.e., the key) and the remaining fields provide relevant data about it.

2) The following are processing problems related to sequential files:
   - Because they can only be read sequentially, getting to the millionth record can take some time.
   - Writing to the end of the file may not be the best solution.
   - The only way to alter a record is to read and rewrite the entire file.

3) Characteristics of direct access or random access files include:
   - Offer a variety of ways of directly jumping to a record of interest, allowing access in roughly the same timescale to any record in the file, no matter how large.
   - Requires the file to reside on a magnetic hard disk drive (HDD) or in memory.
   - New data can be inserted within an existing file between previous records.
   - Are more intricate to design than their sequential counterparts and require more complex, careful processing to maintain their internal structure and consistency.

4) Object stores typically provide directly programmable interfaces, a namespace that spans multiple physical hardware instances, and data management functions such as data replication and distribution.

5) Object stores focus on storing massive amounts of unstructured, write-once, read-many data, but may also include tables, queues, and other data structures.

6) Big data drove the need for a file system distributed over multiple disks, thus popularizing the Hadoop Distributed File System, HDFS.

7) This first class of database management systems (DBMS) focused specifically on transaction processing and the need for rapid, reliable access to and updates of specific, individual data items.

8) Some of the issues related to early database management systems are:
   - Database implementations often maintain strong links to the physical data storage structure.
   - While recognizing the business-oriented view, it remains focused on data rather than on information.
   - Access and usage remained in the hands of programmers and database administrators.

9) The major developments of the relational model and relational databases are:
   - The relational model was introduced in 1970. This mathematically based model provided a complete, comprehensive relational algebra describing possible operations on data, as well as mathematically valid outcomes of the operations. The table and row structure made the model understandable by many business users.

- In 1973, the beginnings of a relational database were under development and by the 1980s, several commercially viable databases were available.
- In 1984, a massively parallel database product was released.
- By the 1990's, relational database management systems were the dominant technology for data management.

10) The relational model provides a declarative method for defining data and queries. Data is managed using a structure in which all data is represented in terms of tuples [sequences or ordered lists of elements], grouped into relations. Users (or administrators) state directly the information the database should contain and what information they want to retrieve from it. The responsibility for defining underlying data storage structures and retrieval procedures to answer queries lies with the RDBMS.

11) Relational databases use SQL definitions and query language. Rather than the relational model terms, a relational database uses the terms table, column, row, and value. These terms are very familiar to businesspeople who use spreadsheets.

12) .The three basic concepts that are fundamental to all relational database design are:
- Normalization.
- Primary/foreign key relationships.
- Joins.

13) The types of problems that can be resolved by normalization are:
- Updating data is facilitated since each normalized table contains only information for the specific variable.
- Necessary information can be derived efficiently by joining only the tables containing the needed data.

14) Third normal form (3NF) is usually considered the most efficient and easily maintained format for a database that requires extensive read/write activity—an operational system. User queries requiring multiple joins may require significant processing, which may necessitate different storage, making 3NF less effective.

15) The following describes the ACID model:
- **Atomicity**: Transactions are executed in an "all or nothing" mode; if any part of the transaction fails, the entire transaction is rolled back.
- **Consistency**: Only valid data, according to the database's consistency rules, will be written to the database.
- **Isolation**: Multiple transactions occurring at the same time will not affect one another, implying also that a transaction cannot read data from any other transaction that has not yet completed.
- **Durability**: Any transaction committed to the database is permanent and will never be lost.

16) Problems associated with transaction-oriented databases include:
- The model adds complexity to the internal operations of the relational database management system (RDBMS), especially for informational systems (data warehouses), with the greatest impact during write operations.
- Designed to write in a row-oriented format, these are optimal for row-oriented read/write operations but less effective for set-based operations that might require access to a few columns across all rows.

17) Transaction-oriented relational databases were effective for the enterprise data warehouses (EDWs) of the layered approach, where significant row-based processing is required. But data mart implementations, where much of the query activity occurs, encountered performance challenges that could be mitigated by creating multiple indexes within the tables. However, these indexes created issues with update performance and ongoing maintenance. Dimensional data warehouses were less affected because their structures were better optimized for queries.

18) Relational databases, especially those with good transactional support, are viable platforms for MGD, particularly if volumes and velocities are not excessive.

19) The performance challenges and implementation complexity associated with first-generation RDBMS, combined with the advances in hardware and renewed software thinking, lead to the development of combined hardware/software solutions-analytical appliances or data warehouse appliances.

20) Analytical appliances are optimized for end-use-focused, read-only analytic applications consistent with data marts.

21) Although slower than main memory, SSDs are up to five times faster than HDDs and offer permanent storage of data. It can also emulate an HDD or be attached to the main data bus.

22) Columnar storage arranges the columns of tables sequentially on disk. Since most information work accesses data from a few columns across multiple rows, columnar storage provides significant performance gains compared to data residing on HDDs.

23) Analytical appliances offer lower costs and speedy implementations. However, they create another copy of the data, which has to be loaded into and formatted for the appliance.

24) Two recent trends in analytic appliances are:
   - Hybrid row-column databases in which the database management system can store data in row, column, or both formats as mandated by the database administrator or, in certain circumstances, automatically.
   - Revamping the query plan optimizer. Changes in the hardware environment, such as in-memory storage, SSDs, and the growth of MPP, have resulted in orders-of-magnitude differences in access speed, requiring significant ongoing changes to query plan optimization.

25) Persistent memory adds an additional tier in the storage hierarchy. The speed is similar to that of memory, and the data is non-volatile. This development will drive the evolution of hybrid database functions capable of supporting combined operational/informational use, as well as the rework of internal database functions, including query optimization.

26) The downside of using large numbers of cheap servers is that failure of individual nodes is inevitable, so a fault-tolerant storage approach is required. Files are thus divided into large blocks, with each block of data stored in triplicate across different nodes.

27) HDFS's focus on large-scale batch processing makes it unsuitable for real-time, read/write, or interactive processing, as well as for supporting PMD. Its ability to store and manage large, loosely structured data makes it ideal for HSI.

28) The following are characteristics that may be included in a NoSQL database management system:

- Non-relational.
- Distributed.
- Open-source.
- Horizontally scalable.
- Schema-free.
- Easy replication.
- Simple application programming interface (API).
- Eventually consistent/BASE (not ACID).
- A huge amount of data.

29) For a database management system to be BASE, it must be:
- **Basically available**: Basic read/write operations are widely available across all nodes of a database cluster, but without any guarantee of consistency (writes may not persist, and reads may not reflect the latest write).
- **Soft state**: Because there is no guarantee of consistency, there is only some probability of knowing the state at a later time, as writes across the cluster may not yet have converged.
- **Eventually consistent**: If we wait long enough after any set of writes, we will eventually know the state of the database and further reads will be consistent with our expectations.

30) The NoSQL data stores described in the text are:
- Key-Value Store.
- Wide Column Store.
- Document Store.
- Graphs.

31) The wide-column store is ideal for searching a large collection of web pages and related information.

32) Document stores represent the most evolved form of a key-value store, with each document containing a set of related key-value pairs. They offer a fully general structure of multiple key-value pairs, with every key being indexable. Nested structures representing changes to the original information are also possible.

33) Databases must balance where to put functionality needed for business use: in the DBMS or in the application. The criticism of NoSQL data stores is that functionality has moved more to the application, requiring specialized development skills and potentially delivering it across multiple applications.

34) The two types of graph databases are:
- Labeled Property Graphs (LPG) associate property information—useful characteristics of nodes or edges, such as names, labels, values, and even creation or modification dates—with each node and edge, represented as key-value pairs.
- Resource Description Framework (RDF) triple stores, originally designed to model metadata, have evolved into a more academic, less user-friendly model for representing relationships in the form of subject => predicate => object triples.

35) Object stores manage data as objects, each identified by a globally unique identifier and containing the data itself and a variable amount of metadata/context-setting information. Objects are better than HDFS in terms of scalability, durability, persistence, and price. HDFS performs better due to

optimizations for Hadoop processing. Security and limitations preferences will depend on the specific object store choice.

36) The challenges of such an environment lie less in the database and storage technology than in the data management of a highly disparate, distributed data resource and in the data population technology required to transport it.

95

Information Preparation: Tools and Techniques

Educational Objectives

Upon completion of this assignment, you should be able to:

1. List and define the broad categories of information preparation tools.
2. Describe their evolution in focus and over time.
3. Define extract, transform, and load (ETL) tooling and where it is appropriate.
4. Define data warehouse automation (DWA), data integration suites, and a variety of other common tool categories, as well as their pros and cons.
5. Define data virtualization and streaming, and provide examples of their uses.
6. Describe how information preparation supports data management and data quality.

For each assignment, define or describe each of the Key Terms and Concepts and answer each of the Review and Discussion Questions.

Key Terms and Concepts

Information Preparation:

Data Pipeline:

Information Preparation in Advance:

Bespoke Extract, Transform, and Load Development:

Historicization:

Data Integration:

Data Integration Suites:

Data Warehouse Automation (DWA):

Data Wrangling:

Cloud Information Preparation:

Microservices:

Inflow Information Preparation:

Data Virtualization:

Streaming Solutions:

Review Questions

1) What value did IBM's *Interface to Operational Systems* and its supplement, the *Data Enhancement Manager,* bring to the data/information preparation arena in the 1980s?

2) What was the evolution from bespoke programs and what did this presage?

3) Beginning in the late 2000s, what value did Data Warehouse Automation (DWA) and streaming tools offer?

4) Why has data wrangling become a tool for data scientists and data-savvy businesspeople?

5) How do data pipelines contrast with more integrated design thinking?

6) What is the risk associated with data pipelines?

7) Identify the major challenges in information preparation and potential solutions.

8) What are the questions answered by basic information preparation and what are those answers?

9) What are the advantages of bespoke ETL development?

10) What are the disadvantages of bespoke ETL development?

11) Describe the user interface supporting definition, implementation, maintenance, and upgrade (DIMU).

12) Identify the two approaches used to convert the DIMU developed in CSI to an executable task.

13) Discuss how ETL implementation design affects the consistency of the DIMU and O&M in the ETL lifecycle.

14) Identify the two factors that affect the complexity of the transform function.

15) What types of rules can be applied in conversion?

16) What is the value of aggregation?

17) What are the complications of enrichment applied to multiple records?

18) Describe the process of bulk transfer for information preparation in advance.

19) What is the benefit of bulk transfer? What is the problem with it?

20) Describe the process of a trickle feed for information preparation in advance. What is its benefit over bulk transfer?

21) What is the issue with the process of trickle feed?

22) What is the data management concern with systems that use both bulk transfer and trickle feed?

23) What are the benefits of data integration suites? What are the challenges?

24) How did data warehouse automation improve on data integration suites?

25) What are the benefits of data warehouse automation?

26) What data scientist concerns led to the concept of data wrangling?

27) What are the pros and cons of data wrangling?

28) Given the data management issues related to cloud information preparation tools, where should data managers focus their attention for evaluation?

29) What challenges does the microservices approach present for ETL development and maintenance?

30) What role do data managers need to play as microservices architecture is increasingly deployed?

31) How does inflow information preparation differ from ETL?

32) Identify the two categories of inflow information preparation.

33) Identify the two data virtualization implementation classes and the situations in which they would be used.

34) What are the data management challenges associated with data virtualization?

35) What are the issues raised by streaming?

36) What are the data management concerns related to streaming?

37) What are the data management takeaways from the discussion of information preparation tools?

Discussion Questions

NOTE: The questions below are intended to continue to challenge you to test your knowledge of the required reading by applying what you have studied to real-life situations.

No suggested answers are provided at the end of the assignment for these types of open discussion questions. Answers may vary by student and will depend on their organization's culture, resources, and processes.

1) What types of information preparation tools are in use at your organization?

2) How has your organization addressed some of the limitations of information preparation tools?

Answers to Assignment 7 Questions

NOTE: These answers are provided to give students a basic understanding of acceptable types of responses. They are often not the only valid answers and are not intended to provide an exhaustive response to the questions.

Key Terms and Concepts

Information Preparation: A process that stores (or loads) its output in a database or other data structure where it can be used and reused by the business as needed.

Data Pipeline: A managed, end-to-end sequence of processes that collect, modify, and deliver data from one or more sources to a target.

Information Preparation in Advance: A process to create and maintain a second (often modified) copy of the data before the business needs it, best characterized by extract, transform, and load.

Bespoke Extract, Transform, and Load Development: Programmer-written code to open file/database, read data, manipulate as required, write resulting data to file/database, repeat as required.

Historicization: Database update process in which deleted records are flagged as no longer current but left in place; changed records are flagged as no longer current, and the new version is inserted in the table. This approach is generally implemented as bitemporal data.

Data Integration: A synonym for the full scope of the term information preparation.

Data Integration Suites: A natural outgrowth of the basic information preparation function, which may include data virtualization, data catalog, and data meaning discovery, data quality and cleansing functions, supported by AI automation and augmentation, in an all-encompassing platform for data management and preparation.

Data Warehouse Automation (DWA): A broader view of data integration suites from information preparation alone to the entire lifecycle of data warehouse design, development, operation, maintenance, and upgrade, to automate the full process as far as possible, often with improved business involvement in the design phase.

Data Wrangling: A category of information preparation tools usually with simple spreadsheet-like user interfaces that generate transformation rules to automate the process, often in the context of collaborative work among data science groups.

Cloud Information Preparation: Represents a reversion to the approach of providing information preparation on a server, often in the cloud, independent of the source and target data stores.

Microservices: This architectural style structures an application as a collection of services that address small, well-bounded business capabilities. These structures are independently deployable, loosely coupled, and owned and maintained by a small team.

Inflow Information Preparation: Offers just-in-time delivery of the required data as the business requests it.

Data Virtualization: Inflow information preparation tools that address the logical, REAL architecture reification component of the digital information systems architecture (DISA). Also known as data federation or enterprise information integration (EII).

Streaming Solutions: An inflow preparation tool that applies to events, measures, and messages that are generated either on the Internet of Things (IoT) or internally to the enterprise. Also called complex event processing (CEP).

Review Questions

1) The *Interface to Operational Systems* provided a concept of an integrated, metadata- and rules-driven system that managed and orchestrated the process of obtaining data and its definitions from operational systems as snapshots or changes, and loading them into or updating the data warehouse. The Data Enhancement Manager provided guidance for data consolidation and enrichment on arrival in the data warehouse.

2) The evolution from bespoke systems was for the internal IT department to design and build a generic interface and enhancement system. Although internally developed, this system presaged the emergence of vendor-developed Extract, Transform, and Load (ETL) tools in the mid-1990's.

3) Beginning in the late 2000s, Data Warehouse Automation (DWA) and streaming tools offered the following value:
   - DWA offered ease of use, full lifecycle support for the data warehouse, and a lower price.
   - Streaming tools supported the volume of data across the Internet and IOT by handling multiple feeds, ensuring consistency, and transferring data on the fly.

4) Data scientists and other businesspeople couldn't wait for IT to develop the means to perform basic data cleansing, manipulation, and loading, so they developed the processes themselves.

5) In contrast to more integrated design thinking, each pipeline focuses on specific data delivery needs.

6) The risk associated with pipelines is a return to the highly siloed development approaches to populating early warehouses.

7) The major challenges of information preparation and their possible solutions are:
   - Lack of real business involvement can be reduced by lowering the barrier for collaboration between businesspeople and IT, as well as involving the business on an ongoing basis in the design and maintenance of information preparation solutions is necessary.
   - Agile development methodologies can remedy slow reaction to new data sources.
   - Lack of agility in deployment that can leave business without access to needed data can be improved through the use of Agile development methodologies.
   - Slow delivery, which impacts real-time business needs, must be addressed by information preparation tools that meet requirements without sacrificing quality or auditability.

- Poor or mixed data quality coming from multiple sources must be recognized and addressed.

8) Basic information preparation asks questions and provides answers:
   - Given a data store in one location, how do we provide a valid version, subset, or derivation of it in a second location and for a different purpose? The answer is to make a copy, modify as needed, and store it somewhere for later (and repeated) use.
   - What to do when the source data changes? The answer is to repeat the original, modify it, store it, and process it.

9) Bespoke development is generally the fastest and easiest approach to ETL. Furthermore, it is generally straightforward to design and build these programs/scripts; most IT departments have the skills to do so; the programs/scripts can be optimized precisely to the existing IT environment and the required data and transformation needs; and the results can be delivered relatively quickly to the business.

10) Over time, many programs/scripts are developed to perform similar operations on data from the same source, based on different interpretations of the underlying data or their transformations. The software environment becomes unmanageable, so that changes in requirements for new, previously uncaptured data, new transformations on existing data, or changes to source systems require reanalysis, redesign, and recoding of an unknown number of programs. This threatens data quality and auditability.

11) The tools offer a graphical user interface in which users drag and drop predefined source, target, and transformation widgets onto a canvas and link them to form a complete information preparation flow, which is stored in CSI and later converted into executable tasks.

12) The two approaches used to convert the DIMU stored as CSI to executable tasks are:
   - In code generation, the logic is converted into a standard programming language, such as COBOL, compiled, and run.
   - A software engine can be built to interpret the rules/metadata at runtime and execute the required function on an intermediate, specialized information preparation server.

13) The co-location of DIMU with transformation on a preparation server offers improved focus on data quality and lineage issues compared to the co-location of extract and DIMU, where generated code on the source server can be easily edited separately from the CSI maintained elsewhere. However, in both cases, operation and maintenance (O&M) has no direct link to DIMU, which can also affect data quality. DIMU, transform, and O&M co-located on the target server is the most effective for consistency.

14) Two factors that affect the complexity of the transform function are:
   - The relationship between the number of input and output records.
   - The type of computation applied at a field level within the records.

15) The types of rules that can be applied in conversion are:
   - A formula is simple logic or math contained within the conversion process itself.
   - A lookup table supports a broader set of relationships between input and output, and the possibility to easily extend the set over time.

16) Aggregation results in a considerable reduction in the number of records which is good for storage volumes, performance, or ease of use. The information content is also reduced, thus limiting unforeseen future uses of the data.

17) In many multi-record cases, one cannot assume that the fields to be combined are simultaneously available. At a technical level, this may simply be a result of the order in which extract jobs run against different source files in batch-processing streams.

18) In a bulk transfer, a snapshot of the current data is extracted from the source when it is deemed internally consistent. For an initial load, it is added to an empty table. If the table already exists, it is overwritten, or records may be added to the end of the file.

19) Bulk transfer is the earliest preferred approach in ETL since it offers the highest guarantee of consistency between source and target data. However, if only a few records need to be updated, bulk transfer may be inefficient, posing problems for network traffic and database performance.

20) Trickle feed is a record-by-record update that can be more efficient than a bulk transfer if only a few records need to be updated. Records to be changed or deleted are identified through various methods called change capture and replication. The changes are applied to the captured records. There are several ways this occurs, depending on the level of history required in the target database. Changed or deleted records in the source can be reflected exactly the same way in the target, or by historicization.

21) Identifying the records that need updating or deleting can be a challenge. Still, processes have been developed to handle this problem that depend on the amount of history the database needs to maintain.

22) The existence of two different feeds can cause data quality and consistency problems. Operational systems may have been designed with end-of-day processes that correct, extend, integrate, or otherwise manipulate data that has been entered during the business day. Any intra-day transfers may contain incomplete or unintegrated data, which cannot be logically combined with data already in the target. If no workarounds are possible, intra-day data may have to carry "public health warnings" in the form of CSI/metadata for businesspeople who use it.

23) The interrelated nature of data integration suites provides consistent metadata/CSI, resulting in cost savings. However, the focus is often too IT-centric, and the initial CSI gathered is often technical in nature. The software is perceived by some as expensive, and the ongoing support expense may be judged too high.

24) Data warehouse automation, enabled by improved RDBMS performance, allowed the transformation to be moved from a separate server, as is typical in data integration suites, to the database server.

25) In addition to saving the cost of a dedicated server for transformation, the cost of IT support staff is reduced due to the simplified, automated data warehouse lifecycle. The streamlined process may encourage businesses to be more involved in design, resulting in faster delivery of functions through Agile development methods. DWA tools often automatically generate design documentation to aid later lineage tracing and impact analysis of changes required as business needs evolve or source systems change.

26) Data scientists were spending as much as 80% of their time cleansing and preparing data for their analytic work. This led to a simpler approach to data preparation in data wrangling, data munging, and data janitoring.

27) Data wrangling is designed to facilitate collaborative work among sophisticated business users. However, it cannot provide transformations for every conceivable need, which requires programmer exits and makes it less user-friendly. An additional problem may arise when moving from data science R&D to an IT-managed environment, requiring the rewriting of transformation scripts. Furthermore, the move from data wrangling to analysis can be cyclical: wrangling to analysis, wrangling to analysis, wrangling to analysis. Data quality and management issues can arise during both the cycling and the transition to an IT-managed environment.

28) Data managers should focus on the overall integrity of the information preparation environment proposed by IT, tailored to the specific circumstances of your environment.

29) This approach may result in fragmentation, causing a constant game of catch-up with source application changes.

30) Data managers should carefully monitor the data quality implications for downstream systems. Of concern is the ongoing tradeoff between timeliness and consistency.

31) Unlike ETL, where most data is extracted, transformed, and loaded into a target data store, for inflow information preparation, only the minimum data required by the requestor is extracted, and transformations are applied on the fly.

32) The two categories of inflow information preparation include:
   - Data virtualization, which operates on stored data.
   - Streaming, which operates on data in flight.

33) The two data virtualization implementation classes and the situations in which they would be used are:
   - In-database implementation would be preferred where the majority of an enterprise's data resides in one database environment because it reduces the level of cross-platform data transfer.
   - A dedicated server implementation is more popular and powerful, given the disparate nature of most enterprise data environments today.

34) The data management challenges associated with data virtualization are:
   - Can the specific data be a truly integrated inflow? A common or enterprise data model is needed to ensure consistency.
   - How does timing affect the quality of the inflow data? Directly accessing data from an operational system during the day can lead to inconsistency between the warehouse and operational sources.

35) Issues raised by streaming include:
   - The cost of storage, even on cheap commodity servers, vs. the value of the data collected in such detail and at such speed.
   - Interpreting the data. Is a change an indicator of an important aspect of the thing being measured or a failure by the sensor?
   - The ability to combine data from different streams confidently while it is in-flight.

36) Data management concerns related to streaming include:
   - Consistency concerns related to the three distinct delivery patterns required by the business: at most once, at least once, and exactly once.

- Erroneous results from the complexity of timing and synchronization within and across streams in real time.
- Current products do not cover the entire process, so bespoke programming is needed to provide a complete solution.
- Solutions may include a combination of batch and stream processing, often called a lambda architecture, which demands a deep understanding of how the data is processed on these different paths at different times.

37) The data management takeaways from the discussion of information preparation tools are:
- Information preparation via an integrated, well-designed environment or platform is far more conducive to data management goals than a custom-built set of programs/scripts that evolve over time, although the latter may deliver data earlier and more cheaply in the short term.
- Modern information preparation environments often deliver the same or related data through different approaches: bulk and trickle feed in advance and via data virtualization or streaming. Where these multiple paths exist, data managers should carefully check for data consistency, in meaning and/or timing.
- The metadata created by the design and operation of information preparation tools is a significant subset of the context-setting information of the organization, particularly when it comes to data lineage and cross-source relationships. It must be combined with real business CSI for data management to take full advantage of it.

Information and Data Use by Business

Educational Objectives

Upon completion of this assignment, you should be able to:

1. Define and describe the axes of the DISA people thinking space and their role in understanding human thinking and behavior in decision making.
2. Discuss the Cynefin framework for sensemaking.
3. Describe three types of information use in business: information-centric, process-centric, and collaborative.
4. Discuss the information-centric classes of tooling: BI, analytics, and AI/ML, and compare their strengths and weaknesses.
5. Understand the role of process-centric information use and the consequences of its absence.
6. Discuss how organizational issues influence information use in business.
7. Define the adaptive decision cycle and describe how it overcomes the problems of overly controlled data warehousing and unrestrained spreadsheeting.
8. Describe how data managers can make a positive contribution to information use by business.

For each assignment, define or describe each of the Key Terms and Concepts and answer each of the Review and Discussion Questions.

Key Terms and Concepts

DISA People Thinking Space:

Insightful Decision Making:

Cynefin Framework:

Business Intelligence or Basic Insights:

Analytics:

Artificial Intelligence/Machine Learning:

Review Questions

1) Identify the three axes of the DISA people thinking space and their purpose.

2) Describe the three components of the organizational axis in the DISA people thinking space.

3) The information intent axis of the DISA people thinking space provides the primary linkage from the people space to the information and process spaces below it. Which of the following is NOT true of components of this axis?
   A. Active intent means getting something done, especially in day-to-day operations and in time-constrained or highly driven activities.
   B. Decisive intent means reaching a decision and is seen most obviously in people to whom an organization grants the right to make operational decisions.
   C. Sense-making intent leads to the behavior of seeking a story to explain a phenomenon and to determine what to do about it.
   D. Innovative intent drives the ah-ha moments that move us to the creation of novelty, the spark for new products or processes.

4) BI and analytics can be used to support all of the components of the information intent axis of the DISA people thinking space, except:
   A. Active intent.
   B. Decisive intent.
   C. Sense-making.
   D. Innovative intent.

5) Identify the four components of the psychosocial mindset axis in the DISA people thinking space.

6) How does the logical/rational thinking component of the psychosocial mindset axis of the DISA people thinking space affect decision making?

7) How does the empathic/social thought component of the psychosocial mindset axis of the DISA people thinking space affect decision making?

8) What lesson does the psychosocial axis of the DISA people thinking space offer to data managers?

9) True or False? The Cynefin framework references the idea that all decisions are rooted in the ideal environment.

10) The domains of the Cynefin framework include all of the following except:
    A. Complex
    B. Clear
    C. Complete
    D. Chaotic.

11) For the domains in the Cynefin framework, identify the suggested decision-making behaviors.

12) Compare and contrast the value of BI, analytics, and content/text analysis.

13) Identify the two classes of business intelligence.

14) When did ad hoc querying become a mainstream of business activity?

15) Compare business intelligence (BI) and analytics.

16) Identify how analytics have been used in the insurance industry.

17) How does the Internet of Things (IoT) as a source of analytics data complicate data management?

18) How is the vendor trend toward offering complete solutions that include built-in access to multiple data sources and embedded information-preparation products challenging data management?

19) Which of the following is an approach to artificial intelligence/machine learning?
    A. Artificial neural networks use raw data to discover patterns or correlations.
    B. Supervised learning enables identified patterns to be applied to real-world objects based on previously labeled data, which is an expensive, time-consuming human task to create.
    C. Generative adversarial networks are mathematical models based on the structure of the brain, requiring large sets of training data in an initial learning phase.
    D. Reinforcement learning uses two networks working against one another: one to generate random samples similar to real-world objects and a second to distinguish between real and fake objects.

20) From a business and government point of view, what is the problem with AI/ML algorithms?

21) True or False? AI/ML provides decision-making support solely through automation.

22) True or False? AI/ML can handle more complex conditions than BI and has the prospect of the algorithm learning about new possibilities as the underlying data evolves.

23) How can AI/ML support data management goals?

24) How does augmentation of human cognition support decision-making?

25) How are the two AL/MI approaches of automation and augmentation combined to support business?

26) Why do financial considerations limit the combined use of the two AL/MI approaches of automation and augmentation to support business?

27) What are the consequences of the increasing use of AI/ML in business?

28) What is the role for data managers in evaluating vendor software for BI, analytics, and AI/ML?

29) Describe the process of information use.

30) Describe the search and respond approach to performance management. What is the weakness of this approach?

31) Describe the phases of the monitor, evaluate, decide, and act of the MEDA approach.

32) Identify the tools used for each phase of the MEDA approach.

33) What limits the effectiveness of MEDA, and why does this matter?

34) In the people thinking space of the DISA, decision cycles are concerned with the process between when an event of interest occurs and the decision of how to act. Which of the following is NOT true of the center-out decision cycle?
   A. It is preferred by business analysts.
   B. It is favored by large and highly structured or regulated businesses, such as insurance.
   C. It favors control, consistency, stability, and quality.
   D. It is information-centric and strongly rational in approach.

35) Describe the steps of the center-out decision cycle used by the business to reach a decision.

36) What are the implicit data management considerations inherent in the center-cut decision cycle?

37) Identify the characteristics of edge-on decision cycle.

38) True or False? The edge-on decision cycle modifies the steps of the center-out cycle, replacing the condition step with the innovation step, thus allowing business people to create, combine, and modify data themselves or with support from peers as needed to solve the problem or address the opportunity at hand.

39) How does the innovate step of the edge-on cycle compare to the condition step of the center-out decision cycle?

40) What is the organizational issue with the traditional, center-out data warehouse and BI environment, and how does the adaptive decision cycle resolve it?

41) What is the organizational issue with the edge-on approach?

42) What is the concern with information use in the people thinking space and what role do data managers have in addressing this concern?

Discussion Questions

NOTE: The questions below are intended to continue to challenge you to test your knowledge of the required reading by applying what you have studied to real-life situations.

No suggested answers are provided at the end of the assignment for these types of open discussion questions. Answers may vary by student and will depend on their organization's culture, resources, and processes.

1) How are BI, analytics, and AI/ML used in your organization? What tools are in use?

2) How has your organization addressed the people information space?

Answers to Assignment 8 Questions

NOTE: These answers are provided to give students a basic understanding of acceptable types of responses. They are often not the only valid answers and are not intended to provide an exhaustive response to the questions.

Key Terms and Concepts

DISA People Thinking Space: Provides the foundation for understanding why and how businesspeople use and process information to meet business needs, get their jobs done, and succeed in their roles, both professionally and personally.

Insightful Decision Making: Decision making that is well-informed but also cognizant of the decision maker's mental landscape.

Cynefin Framework: A conceptual aid to sense making and decision making that complements the people thinking space.

Business Intelligence or Basic Insights: An ability to extract from information/data an understanding of the fundamentals of business operations and pose simple, well-bounded questions about trends or exceptions.

Analytics: Statistically based methods, modeling techniques, and algorithms developed in response to growing data volumes.

Artificial Intelligence/Machine Learning: Sophisticated algorithms that discover or "learn" to recognize patterns or correlations in large datasets in support of decision making.

Review Questions

1. The three axes of the DISA people thinking space and their purpose are:
    - **Organizational Role:** People use information and make decisions aligned with their role in the organization.
    - **Psychosocial Mindset:** Insightful decision making seamlessly combines left- and right-brain thinking, taking account of intuitive and emotional responses to reach an integrated, well-rounded position on the decision at hand.
    - **Information/Intent:** Provides the primary link between the people space and the information and process spaces below it.

2. The three components of the organizational axis in the DISA people thinking space can be described:
    - Corporate decisions occur at the highest levels, generally apply across much of the organization and are often strategic in nature.

- The team role applies to all intermediate levels of the organization, including divisions and empowered teams. Much of the decision making is tactical, related to implementing strategy, managing and measuring performance, and tracking down problems.
- At the personal level, individual goals related to business performance and individual personal/professional aims are tracked and problems are addressed.

3. The correct answer choice is B.

4. The correct answer choice is D.

5. The four components of the psychosocial mindset axis in the DISA people thinking space are:
   - Reactive/Emotive impulses.
   - Logical/Rational thinking.
   - Intuitive/Integrative thought.
   - Empathic/Social thought.

6. Although logical/rational thinking is often considered the most desirable and prevalent mode of thinking, logic alone can miss the bigger picture and lead to distinctly inhuman conclusions.

7. Empathic/social thought is the foundation of relating at the personal, group, and societal levels. Collaboration springs from here, and with it, our best opportunities for innovation.

8. Data managers are advised to look beyond pure data-driven thinking to consider how to support businesspeople in making insightful decisions.

9. The statement is False.

10. The correct answer choice is C.

11. Suggested decision-making behaviors for the domains in the Cynefin framework are:
    - **Clear**: Sense the situation, categorize the options, and then apply best practice.
    - **Complicated**: Sense the situation, analyze the options, respond with good practice.
    - **Complex**: Probe, sense, then respond with emergent practice.
    - **Chaotic**: Act, sense, respond with novel practice.

12. BI remains a key component of all ongoing management reporting and basic problem-solving across all lines of business and industries. Analytics, including machine learning and AI, is more exploratory in nature than BI, characterized by the discovery of previously unknown insights in large datasets. Content/text analytics can be viewed as a specific case of analytics and machine learning focused on non-numerical data, including social media.

13. The two classes of business intelligence are:
    - Printed reports satisfy the need for regular, consistent, and comparable information about the ongoing performance of business processes.
    - Ad hoc queries address management needs for troubleshooting and problem determination.

14. Ad hoc query in mainstream corporate computing only became possible with the popularization of relational databases in the mid- to late 1980s, accessed via the SQL language.

15. Business intelligence (BI) and analytics differ in the following ways:

- BI looks to investigate the known, while analytics is searching for the unknown.
- BI uses simple queries on complex data, while analytics uses complex queries on simple data.
- BI requires high-quality, restructured data that hides operational complexity in a simplified view, while analytics requires cleansed raw data at high speed and scale.
- BI relies on information preparation in advance, while analytics relies on manual, on-the-fly information preparation.

16. Common use cases for analytics include fraud detection and prevention, customer retention, detailed risk assessment, personalizing policy offers, and streamlining internal processes, such as speeding up the settlement of complex claims. Mining of social media posts can be used to validate or deny claims. Driving data from pay-as-you-go automobile insurance can be analyzed to personalize insurance packages and reward or penalize drivers as appropriate. Smart home devices offer yet another source of directly useful information to insurers.

17. Much of the data collected by the IoT is repetitive, so transferring it to data centers would be expensive and of little value for analytics. Devices that capture IoT data are enabled to perform preliminary analytics locally, transferring the results and, for more limited volumes of interesting data, more data for centralized analysis. The models on edge devices must be managed alongside the data/information themselves.

18. These functions can lead to the creation of direct links to the database, which bypass data warehouses and data marts where the data quality has been assured. The data manager must be aware of this trend and prepared to challenge approaches that compromise data quality.

19. The correct answer is B: Supervised learning enables identified patterns to be applied to real-world objects based on previously labeled data, which is an expensive, time-consuming human task to create.

20. Many of these algorithms act as "black boxes" where the rationale behind their outcomes is unknown and, in some cases, unknowable. In business and government, such a lack of transparency is generally unacceptable when people's lives may be adversely affected by incorrect outcomes.

21. The statement is False: AI/ML supports decision-making through both automating decision-making and augmenting human cognition in the process of moving from data to decisions.

22. The statement is True.

23. AI can also automate the discovery of metadata/context-setting information in the information preparation process.

24. Augmentation interacts with businesspeople to make sense of complex data in context by exposing insights that they might miss and proposing alternative solutions.

25. Automation takes care of simpler, more straightforward decisions, freeing humans to focus on more complex cases where their natural strengths in innovation or ethical reasoning are most valuable, and where AI can augment them in applying those skills.

26. The immediate cost savings from automation, accruing from staff reductions rather than reassignments, are often valued over potential but future benefits of innovation or ethical decision making.

27. This will lead to reductions in staff engaged in decision making and a shift in their skills. From a data management perspective, data quality problems will be less likely to be detected before data is used. Data managers will need to be more involved in information preparation to maintain or improve data quality.

28. Since product vendors across all three classes blur the boundaries as they try to extend their markets, data managers should keep the quite different information uses at the forefront of their minds when reviewing business information use programs and practices.

29. The process should be a closed loop, beginning with gathering the right information, analyzing and interpreting it, reaching conclusions, making decisions, implementing those decisions, and finally confirming that the action had the desired effect.

30. The search-and-respond approach is appealing for its simplicity. When a change in the external or internal environment is sensed, the business applies intelligence to determine what to do, then responds. The weakness of the approach is that these steps get something done, but to learn from the experience, a feedback loop must be added to create a closed-loop process.

31. The phases of the monitor, evaluate, decide, and act of the MEDA approach include:
    - **Monitor**: The ongoing process of observing what is happening in the environment, both within and without the enterprise.
    - **Evaluate**: When any change is observed, the implications are assessed, consequences gauged, and possible actions evaluated.
    - **Decide**: Based on the outcome of the evaluation, decision makers compare and discuss recommended courses of action and choose the most appropriate.
    - **Act**: The decision is communicated to the enterprise and acted upon.

32. The tools used for each phase of the MEDA approach are:
    - **Monitor**: Traditional operational systems, including dashboards and portals, as well as external big data sources.
    - **Evaluate**: Traditional informational systems, BI and analytics tools, and increasingly AI.
    - **Decide**: Face-to-face meetings and the use of collaborative tools characterize this phase.
    - **Act**: Collaborative tools, possibly leading to changes in behaviors, measures, or entire processes, and, in the more extreme cases, the design of operational and informational systems.

33. Because the tools to support the feedback process are lacking, businesses often can't compare the expected and actual outcomes of their decisions and actions. This matters since understanding the correlation or lack thereof between actions and outcomes becomes increasingly important as sophisticated analytics or black-box AI systems offer non-intuitive solutions to new problems or opportunities.

34. The correct answer choice is A.

35. The steps of the center-out decision cycle used by the business to reach a decision include:
    - **Garner**: The raw and atomic data about business events and their status is collected and stored in a data warehouse designed and run by IT.
    - **Condition**: Derived data is generated by cleansing, combining, filtering, and enriching raw and atomic data, also in the warehouse.
    - **Utilize**: The recorded and conditioned data is then used to make decisions using BI tools.

- **Iterate**: Learning from the use made of the data and any issues encountered, any changes to the data needed by the process are applied by IT and returned to the garner step.

36. Data management, supported by IT, perceives this model as key to achieving and maintaining data quality and auditability. This model assumes that there exists a central authority, often data management in concert with the data warehouse team, that knows users' needs and asserts control over the data content and how it is manipulated in the garner, condition, and iterate steps. Also implicit is the belief in a largely unidirectional progression from raw data to final use.

37. The characteristics of the edge-on decision cycle are:
    - Named for the way in which data originates and circulates on the edge of the organization, often in spreadsheets.
    - Originates with businesspeople who gather data from all sources, including spreadsheets.
    - Focuses on immediate problem solving and operates on a shorter timeframe than traditional BI.
    - Supports innovation and change.
    - Is more people-oriented and supports the intuitive and social.
    - Is preferred by businesspeople.

38. The statement is True.

39. Condition and innovate are similar, differing in intent and location. In innovation, business people process data to improve its usefulness in decision making. In the condition step, IT processes the data to improve the quality of its content. These are complementary aims and actions, as are the two cycles themselves.

40. Traditional, center-out systems begin and are defined at the corporate level, then promulgated down to team and personal levels. However, often corporate doesn't know what the front line needs, frustrating the business's ability to innovate by requiring them to return to IT time and again for new and improved data. The adaptive cycle encourages exploration, peer review, and promotion through formal procedures, so that the resulting routines can be officially implemented for stability and quality.

41. While errors and the lack of auditability with spreadsheets, a central tool of the edge-on approach, are certainly problematic, the real problem is the way they are promoted throughout the organization without IT or data management involvement. The lack of checks for data validity, basic data quality, and production readiness leads to errors.

42. Comprehensive data quality work in the information space can be rapidly contaminated and corrupted in the people thinking space if control over information use and promotion is absent or poorly implemented across the organization. Data managers must take a leading role in addressing these challenges and proposing solutions.

Tools and Techniques for Managing Data/Information

Educational Objectives

Upon completion of this assignment, you should be able to:

1. Explain why the data, information, knowledge, wisdom (DIKW) model is no longer useful.
2. Define the manifest meaning model (m^3) and position context-setting information (CSI) in it.
3. Describe why m^3 is important for data management and how it disrupts the concept of a single version of the truth.
4. Explain the evolution of data modeling and its limitations.
5. Describe the modern three-layered modeling approach and the role of graph notation.
6. Define bitemporal data and explain its importance to data management.
7. Describe how semantics and ontology are driving more meaningful information.
8. Define data catalogs and explain how they support data and information management.
9. Explain how master data management (MDM) relates to digital transformation.

For each assignment, define or describe each of the Key Terms and Concepts and answer each of the Review and Discussion Questions.

Key Terms and Concepts

Data, Information, Knowledge, Wisdom (DIKW) Model:

Manifest Meaning Model:

Knowledge:

Explicit Knowledge:

Tactic Knowledge:

Single Source of Truth (SSOT):

Business Concept Model:

Solution Data Model:

Bitemporal Data:

Semantic Web:

Ontology:

Review Questions

1) Describe the structure of the manifest meaning model (m^3).

2) How does information from the physical locus lead to knowledge that can be used in decision making in the mental locus of the m^3 model?

3) Where does gut feel fit into the concept of tacit knowledge and decision making?

4) How is interpersonal locus, meaning, reflected in decisions?

5) How does the view of the world change as we move through the levels of the m^3 model?

6) What roles do IT and data management play in the m^3 model?

7) Where does context-setting information (CSI) reside in the manifest meaning model (m^3)?

8) Of the different types of CSI addressed in the m^3, which is the most difficult to capture and which is the most valuable to business?

9) A new aspect of concern about data is criticality. Of the following, which is true about the levels of criticality?
   A. Non-critical data is about 50% of all data in 2020 and is increasing.
   B. Potentially critical data is necessary for continued business operations.
   C. Critical data is necessary for business survival.
   D. Hypercritical data has a direct and immediate impact on human health and well-being.

10) In what way does criticality affect how data is treated by the business?

11) What are some of the challenges data managers face in attempting to reach beyond data and information to meaning and knowledge?

12) What role does m³ require of data managers?

13) What is the role of data managers given that a single version of the truth is not possible?

14) What is the challenge underlying the concept of a single source of truth?

15) Describe the original diagram representation of the entity-relationship model.

16) True or False? Data modeling and Information modeling are different names for the same concept.

17) What challenges does modeling, both information and data, face in the digital transformation environment?

18) How did the move to enterprise-wide systems, such as data warehouses and master data management, challenge data modeling, and what was the response?

19) Identify the two types of industry models used as a starting point for enterprise-wide system design.

20) What is the three-layer modeling approach, and how does it improve on the entity-relationship model?

21) Describe the business concept model.

22) How does the business concept map, a directed graph, support understanding of business needs?

23) Describe the business terms model alternative to the business concept map.

24) Challenges to the business concepts model include:
    A. Strict language formation.
    B. Deregulation.
    C. Over-hyped expectations of constantly changing technology.
    D. Understated business expectation.

25) Challenges to the business concept and business terms models can be addressed by:
    A. Defining only what is required for the top-level model.
    B. Eliminating ambiguity in definitions of elements and the relationships between them in terms of context, state, time, and motive.
    C. Setting scope in stages to deliver achievable, timely, and valuable results that are stepping stones to a broader, ultimately enterprise-wide outcome.
    D. All of the above are approaches to address the challenges of these models.

26) How does the solution data model relate to the physical data model?

27) The steps in the high-level, top-down process of data/information modeling are:
    A. Subset the scope, elicit business input, extend with operational information, transform into other structures, and optimize.
    B. Elicit business input, subset the scope, extend with operational information, transform into other structures, and optimize.
    C. Subset the scope, elicit business input, extend with operational information, transform into other structures, optimize, and implement.
    D. Elicit business input, subset the scope, extend with operational information, transform into other structures, optimize, and implement.

28) True or False? Bitemporal data does not allow data revisions when needed by the business.

29) How does bitemporal data support data management and governance?

30) How do fully automated audit procedures improve auditability?

31) Why is defining and agreeing on meaning the primary challenge of information/data modeling?

32) True or False? ACORD and IBM proprietary models provide insurance industry standards models.

33) Which of the following are true of industry models?
    A. The strength of these models is that they enable faster project startup and achieve greater cross-organizational consistency than traditional approaches.
    B. The weakness is that the complete model may be so complex that businesspeople may struggle to understand it.
    C. Another weakness is that novel or unique aspects of a business process may be missed in the detail of the generic process.
    D. All of the above are true.

34) What is the role of the data manager in utilizing industry models?

35) From a data management perspective, why are a data-centric approach and semantic/ontological methods imperative in a digital business?

36) What are the data quality concerns and expectations of a digital business?

37) All of the following are context-setting information historically supported in data warehouse environments except:
    A. Data dictionaries containing definitions of data from operational system sources.
    B. Collaboration-based information, such as expertise sources, peers, and informal documentation.
    C. Business process definitions that had been documented in free-form text.
    D. A business data directory as a component of the data warehouse to make the CSI available to business users in the environment.

38) Why have the attempts to develop tools to collect, store, and deliver CSI failed?

39) What is the focus of data catalogs?

40) How do data catalogs support data management, governance, risk, and compliance?

41) True or False? Master data is fairly unstable data comprised of external data.

42) How does master data management (MDM) contribute to the success of a digital business undertaking?

Discussion Questions

NOTE: The questions below are intended to continue to challenge you to test your knowledge of the required reading by applying what you have studied to real-life situations.

No suggested answers are provided at the end of the assignment for these types of open discussion questions. Answers may vary by student and will depend on their organization's culture, resources, and processes.

1. Does your company have an enterprise-wide data model? If so, what tools were used to develop it? An industry model? A data catalog?

2. What data model approach is in use in your company? Entity-Relationship? Manifest Meaning Model? How would a different model improve data management and governance?

Answers to Assignment 9 Questions

NOTE: These answers are provided to give students a basic understanding of acceptable types of responses. They are often not the only valid answers and are not intended to provide an exhaustive response to the questions.

Key Terms and Concepts

Data, Information, Knowledge, Wisdom (DIKW) Model: A model that attempts to define how people internalize and adapt the information they receive and move toward decisions.

Manifest Meaning Model: A conceptual model of the relationships between data/information, knowledge, and meaning, which improves on the DIKW model. The model is denoted as m^3.

Knowledge: Exists only in the human mind and emerges through lifelong exposure to information in all forms and the experience of the reality of cause and effect, personal engagement, and so on.

Explicit Knowledge: An understanding of current or pre-existing internalized information or situation and an ability to access, integrate, and even document it directly in a usable form.

Tactic Knowledge: In decision making, it equates to the insight one has into the information or characteristics of a situation that goes beyond the explicit physical information that is immediately or previously evidently available.

Single Source of Truth (SSOT): Refers to the practice of structuring data models and stores such that every data element is mastered in only one place.

Business Concept Model: One of the models within the three-layer modeling approach, it is a pure business-facing representation that depicts the terminology and structure of information, and its use, as perceived and described by businesspeople.

Solution Data Model: One of the models within the three-layer modeling approach is the representation used by data modelers to understand and document the business concepts and relationships in a more detailed and formal way.

Bitemporal Data: Records the time the event happened in the real world (called valid or application time) and when it was recorded in the database (transaction or system time), in addition to any other business-relevant times.

Semantic Web: Emerging from the semantics communities of the World Wide Web, this is an alternative approach to discerning and documenting meaning, and to allowing automated interpretation and use of the data and information found there.

Ontology: A formal knowledge representation that describes taxonomies and classification networks, providing a structure of knowledge for any domain.

Review Questions

1) The m³ model is presented by three layers or loci:
   - The physical locus is the lowest level of the model and represents data and information. Data and information are distinguished by their structuredness and source. Data is strictly structured, while information is more loosely structured. Data is sourced from the physical world, and information is sourced from the human.
   - The mental locus, the middle level, represents knowledge that is separated into explicit (understanding) and tacit (insight) knowledge.
   - The interpersonal locus, the highest level of the model, represents meaning that reflects the importance of personal relationships and social context in interpreting information and in reaching judgments.

2) Information translates into explicit knowledge or understanding through learning, which can then be fed back into information through documentation. Information translates into tacit knowledge or insight through observation, which can feed information through video. Finally, explicit knowledge through practice becomes tacit knowledge, which can become explicit through articulation.

3) Tacit knowledge includes gut feel. Where data is sparse, unreliable, or even too complicated or extensive for human cognition, gut feel may well be an appropriate or even the only available approach for decision making.

4) It is in this locus that business leaders apply appropriate ethical and societal context to decision making when non-leaders may act with more attention to personal gain and less to social implications.

5) The physical level of data/information reflects an objective/universal view of the world. The interpersonal level, meaning, reflects a subjective/unique view of the world.

6) IT and data managers drive the solution-design iterative process by which business meaning and knowledge are translated into information, followed by data modeling to transform that information into data.

7) CSI, as computer-based information, resides in the physical locus and is composed of loosely and strictly structured data.

8) The know-why aspect of CSI related to the interpersonal locus is the most difficult to capture, since it reflects the interpretations people put on reality, which vary based on an individual's knowledge, experience, and history. It is also among the most valuable to the business, recording the organizational memory of why the solutions that worked did and why those that didn't failed.

9) The correct answer choice is D.

10) Data with higher levels of criticality require more reliable and better performing infrastructure, higher security and privacy, improved business processes, including more rigorous audits, and new legal structures to avoid or mitigate potential and increasing liabilities or, more importantly, loss of life.

11) Some of the challenges data managers face in attempting to reach beyond data and information to meaning and knowledge include:

- Data managers can't get into the heads of businesspeople to truly understand how they use information (explicit and tacit) and interpersonal relationships to make decisions.
- It is difficult for data managers to compete with social and organizational inertia.

12) Data managers need to be involved in teasing out the data and information implications of what is being requested, working closely with the business to understand what is meant by their requirements, which questions need to be answered, and which stories need to be told. They need to explore data definitions and lineage, address data ownership issues, and consider privacy and ethics.

13) A key role for data managers is to understand where and in what context different beliefs and stories about data and information are considered the "one truth," and to ensure that alternative stories are considered.

14) The concept of a single source of truth (SSOT) refers to the practice of structuring data models and stores so that every data element is maintained in only one place. The challenge is to consider what exactly is stored in databases and how they relate to each other.

15) Originally, entities were represented by rectangles. Relationships were represented as triangles and connected to entities via lines. Additional information indicating the cardinality of the relationship between entities was shown by numbers between the entity rectangle and the relationship triangle.

16) The statement is false. Conceptual and logical modeling determine current and future business needs and can be considered information modeling. Physical database design is concerned with what is currently possible and can be considered data modeling.

17) Data and information modeling face the following challenges in the digital transformation environment:
- The implication is that data matters more than information. However, information about what business needs precedes data in the m^3 model. So, at the conceptual and logical level, data is the wrong focus.
- Because of the close relationship between ER modeling and RDB design, developers tend to think too much about RDB implementation too early in the design process.

18) The challenge for data modeling posed by enterprise-wide systems is that user requirements have become broader, more conflicting, and more vague. The response was to use generic, well-proven industry models as a starting point.

19) The two types of industry models used as a starting point for enterprise-wide system design are:
- Top-down models begin with an industry-wide model and customize it to a specific company's needs. it is optimal when cross-enterprise consistency is a priority.
- Bottom-up modeling is appropriate when data source systems already exist or are being redeveloped and strongly drive the system design. Dimensional data warehouses follow this approach.

20) The three-layer model provides separate models for business concepts, solution data, and physical data. Each of these models is appropriate for its audience, improving communication and preventing the collapse of the ER levels into a single model.

21) The business concept model is a pure business-facing representation, depicting the terminology and structure of information and its use as perceived and described by businesspeople, presented as a

directed graph or map that provides intuitive, visual communication of semantically defined business concepts.

22) The business concept map is sufficient to understand and describe the business information needs and relationships in some detail.

23) The business terms model depends on the development of a common business language presented in the crow's foot style.

24) The correct answer choice is C.

25) The correct answer choice is D.

26) The solution data model can be directly transformed and optimized from the labeled property graph to the physical data model for implementation in any database, including a graph database, or to a detailed entity-relationship model for implementation in a relational database or NoSQL store.

27) The correct answer choice is B.

28) The statement is false. Collecting when events occur and when they are recorded in the warehouse helps manage the warehouse, supports data revisions when needed by the business, and enables businesspeople to run historical queries and track trends.

29) By providing an historical record of data changes within the database itself, auditability is significantly improved, as all additions, changes, and deletions remain in the database and are accessible to auditors in the context of how they occurred.

30) Fully automated audit procedures, or rules-based audits, apply quantitative measures and conditional rules on a regular basis within the database to audit regulatory and compliance requirements across the full contents of the database.

31) An agreement doesn't eliminate all ambiguity. Alternative interpretation can be accepted, and homonyms and synonyms may be identified. As the model expands and more people are involved, the meaning becomes more complex and multifaceted.

32) The statement is False. IBM proprietary models do not provide insurance industry standards.

33) The correct answer choice is D.

34) Data managers, who have a broad understanding of the business concerns and knowledge of data-specific considerations, will play an important role in balancing the pros and cons of using these industry models.

35) Self-describing information is the foundation of a digital business. From a data management perspective, a data-centric approach and semantic/ontological methods offer a means to achieve and maintain data quality, integrity, and security across the enterprise.

36) As data becomes more pervasive, high-speed, and its sourcing automated, historical data quality issues, such as data entry errors, poor application design, increasing data entropy, and a lack of understanding of the data by those who enter it, are amplified and brought to the forefront. In the digital business, the base data must be completely defined, widely understood, and as error-free as possible.

37) The correct answer choice is B.

38) The attempts to develop tools to collect, store, and deliver CSI failed because:
- Few enterprises can calculate the explicit value of the tools or commit the resources to populate them.
- The focus was on the needs of IT and data engineering staff, providing more technical metadata than business context.

39) The focus is on improving the productivity of data scientists, business analysts, and businesspeople in discovering the data they need, understanding what it means, and enabling the reuse of existing data.

40) Data catalogs support data management, governance, risk, and compliance in the following ways:
- For regulatory purposes, catalogs support regulatory requirements for privacy protection.
- Data managers use catalogs to discover information overlaps between systems and to find multiple copies of purchased data.
- Auditors use catalogs to discover and understand data being used in processes of interest and for purposes for which they were not intended.

41) The statement is false. Master data is fairly stable data comprised of an organization's core data, containing the basic information needed to conduct business.

42) MDM focuses on real-time consolidation of master data, an organization's core data, contributing to data quality and consistency. In this way, MDM supports the success of digital business.

Creating an Information-centric Organization

Educational Objectives

Upon completion of this assignment, you should be able to:

1. List the types of challenges faced by typical informational projects and their underlying causes.
2. Describe the difference between programs and projects.
3. Explain the importance and role of the chief executive officer in digital transformation.
4. Describe the roles of chief data, analytics, and digital transformation officers and how they differ.
5. Describe what a center of competence/excellence is.
6. Explain the role, required skills, and responsibilities of the digital business center of excellence (DBCoE).
7. Discuss the pros and cons of bimodal IT as an approach to reorganizing IT for digital transformation.
8. Explain the concept of infonomics and outline its value in digital transformation.
9. Describe how connected architecture offers a new requirement management approach for informational programs such as digital transformation.

For each assignment, define or describe each of the Key Terms and Concepts and answer each of the Review and Discussion Questions.

Key Terms and Concepts

Chief Information Officer (CIO):

Chief Technology Officer (CTO:)

Chief Data Officer (CDO):

Chief Digital Officer (CXO):

Center of Excellence (CoE):

Bimodal:

Infonomics:

Data Culture:

Information Framework:

Connected Architecture:

Review Questions

1) Identify the ten most common attributes found in unsuccessful data warehouse, data lake, big data, and digital transformation initiatives.

2) Identify some data/information delivery problems that result in unsuccessful digital transformation initiatives.

3) True or False? Both traditional application development and digital transformation try to provide an environment in which businesspeople can explore and address their own needs and problems.

4) How does a digital transformation program compare to the data warehouse program?

5) Why is active CEO support of a digital transformation initiative fundamental to success?

6) Identify the three ways the CEO can lead in digital transformation.

7) The common critical, high-level areas where digital transformation can have the most impact or where there is the most need for change include all the following except:
    A. Customer disengagement.
    B. Digital products and services.
    C. Operational performance.
    D. Preparing for disruptive new business models from existing competitors and new platform challengers.

8) How might the CEO drive organizational change?

9) Which of the following are true of the roles and responsibilities of the Chief Information Officer (CIO), Chief Technology Officer (CTO), and Chief Data Officer (CDO)?
    A. The CIO is responsible for IT and focuses on the technology that runs the business's operations. The CIO's responsibility is to reduce IT costs.
    B. In some organizations, the CTO considers future technology developments to support the business's needs. This position is in addition to a CIO.
    C. The recognition of the role and importance of data, regardless of technology, together with the emergence of new data from the internet, led to the emergence of the CDO.
    D. All of the above are true.

10) How does the position of data manager fit into the CIO, CDO, and CDAO structure?

11) Identify the four archetypes of Chief Data Officer leaders and areas of responsibility.

12) Identify the functions of the Chief Digital Officer (CXO).

13) How does the focus of a CIO differ from that of a CXO?

14) All of the following are conditions that wear down the enthusiasm and drive of a new Chief Digital
Officer except:
    A. Organization's resistance to change.
    B. Incomplete documentation of existing systems.
    C. Turf protection in organizational silos.
    D. Slow progress and occasional failures in such a complex program.

15) Why is combining the Chief Data Officer and Chief Digital Officer roles not a good idea?

16) What are the challenges to implementing a digital business?

17) How does the center of excellence (CoE) program management approach support digital
transformation?

18) What skill set is needed by the staff of the DBCoE?

19) List the responsibilities and roles of the digital business center of excellence (DBCoE).

20) True or False? The DBCoE works to define and secure agreement on the overall digital business strategy and its relationship to the corporate strategy, ensuring that the digital business strategy evolves with the business strategy while promoting a vibrant, pervasive data culture.

21) What is the DBCoE role in program design and ongoing management?

22) How does the DBCoE play a leading role in selling digital transformation across the business?

23) What is DBCoE's role in educating and training to support digital transformation?

24) True or False? The DBCoE forces one-way communication between enterprise- and functional-level groups responsible for architecture and governance to ensure the organizational goals are achieved.

25) What conditions of digital transformation underlie the need for bimodal IT?

26) Identify how the two types of bimodal modes are optimized.

27) Identify the characteristics of Mode 1.

28) Identify the characteristics of Mode 2.

29) Why is there an interdependence between mode 1 and mode 2 teams?

30) How does the DBCoE fit into the bimodal IT structure?

31) Which of the following is NOT a process involved in infonomics?
   A. **Monitor:** Continually evaluate existing systems to determine the accuracy, validity, and timeliness of existing information assets.
   B. **Monetize:** Identify why information affords unique opportunities to be monetized directly or indirectly, and how to build a business case for deploying both internally generated and externally sourced information.
   C. **Manage:** From other asset classes, learn the challenges of and how to apply best practices for managing all forms of information as an asset class to create a savvy organization.
   D. **Measure:** Provide specific valuation models to measure information as an asset, address real and perceived impediments, and adapt key economic principles to quantify the various aspects and impact of information assets.

32) Identify the ways information can be monetized directly or indirectly.

33) All of the following are steps to developing an infonomics environment except:
   A. Establish an information strategy or information product function.
   B. Identify ways to generate direct and indirect economic benefits from each asset.
   C. Prepare data and establish the "market" without exploring how others have monetized data.
   D. Gauge success and alter strategy and tactics as appropriate.

34) Identify the purpose of the foundational measures of value of information and list three measures.

35) Financial measures improve the economic benefits of information. Measures include which of the following?
   A. Cost value of information (CVI), which measures what it costs to collect this data, or what would be the cost of losing it.
   B. Market value of information (MVI) measures what the organization could get from selling or trading this data.
   C. Economic value of information (EVI), which measures how this data contributes to revenue or expense savings.
   D. All of the above.

36) How do the foundational and financial measures of infonomics support digital transformation?

37) What is the main reason BI, data warehouse, and digital transformation projects fail?

38) True or False? A strong data culture is the last step in equipping staff with the skills needed to leverage data and contribute to its valorization.

39) Identify the three challenges to defining the information framework.

40) Identify the three layers of the connected architecture and how they interact.

41) How do the roles described in the human interaction layer of the connected architecture differ in practice from the conceptual ideal, and how does this complicate data management?

42) How does the connected architecture provide a management approach for digital transformation?

43) Why is the distinction between information consumers and producers so important?

Discussion Questions

NOTE: The questions below are intended to continue to challenge you to test your knowledge of the required reading by applying what you have studied to real-life situations.

1) What structure does your organization have: CIO, CDO, DBCoE? Where do you fit in the structure? Discuss how they have impacted your role as a data manager.

2) Does your company have a traditional IT department, or has it embraced the bimodal model? How has the structure worked? What challenges have you seen?

Answers to Assignment 10 Questions

NOTE: These answers are provided to give students a basic understanding of acceptable types of responses. They are often not the only valid answers and are not intended to provide an exhaustive response to the questions.

Key Terms and Concepts

Chief Information Officer (CIO): The senior person responsible for IT.

Chief Technology Officer (CTO): The senior person responsible for consideration of future technology needs.

Chief Data Officer (CDO): The senior person, with a business focus, who understands the strategy and direction of the business, but whose focus is on how to underpin that with data and drive business value from it.

Chief Digital Officer (CXO): The senior person responsible for oversight of digital business transformation. May also be called Chief Digital Transformation Officer or Chief Digital Information Officer.

Center of Excellence (CoE): A widely regarded and common approach to program management. Also called the Center of Competence (CoC) or Competency Center.

Bimodal: The practice of managing two separate but coherent styles of work: one focused on predictability; the other on exploration.

Infonomics: The emerging discipline of managing and accounting for information with the same or similar rigor and formality as other traditional assets and liabilities (such as financial, physical, and intangible assets and human capital).

Data Culture: A strategy in which the C-suite drives appropriate behaviors and beliefs across all people in the organization that data is an asset and should be valued, managed, and used as such.

Information Framework: A system capable of defining, delivering, maintaining, and using information based on a collaborative effort, involving all stakeholders in the information value delivery chain, to arrive at a consensus about what the information means, how it can be used, and how its use can change the underlying business process.

Connected Architecture: A framework and thought process for the organization of data warehouses and BI projects that applies equally to digital transformation.

Review Questions

1. The ten most common attributes found in unsuccessful data warehouse, data lake, big data, and digital transformation initiatives include:
    - Not answering the big question: Why?
    - Using the Big Bang approach.
    - Jumping straight into writing code.
    - Treating requirements and deliverables as just checkboxes.
    - Disconnect between technical staff and stakeholders.
    - Shortening (or even skipping entirely) testing and validation.
    - Spending too little time on ETL [extract, transform, and load].
    - Skipping the training.
    - Using the wrong personnel.
    - Neglecting maintenance.

2. Some data/information delivery problems that result in unsuccessful digital transformation initiatives are:
    - Collecting the wrong or unneeded data for the business objectives.
    - Providing users with ill-defined information.
    - Failing to reconcile data from multiple sources to common models, structures, and timing.
    - Delivering data at the wrong time or at the wrong speed.
    - Delivering systems that struggle to respond to rapidly changing business needs.

3. The statement is False. Traditional application development aims to deliver a point solution to a (reasonably) well-defined business need or problem. Informational systems and, indeed, digital business try to provide an environment in which businesspeople can explore and address their own needs and problems.

4. Both share the common characteristic of related projects, although the digital transformation program is on a much greater scale. Unlike a data warehouse program with its single focus, the digital transformation program balances changing business needs and evolving technological possibilities across the organization to deliver a consistent, integrated architecture in easy-to-digest and nourishing chunks.

5. The CEO provides upfront and ongoing clear direction and cross-enterprise prioritization. On an ongoing basis, CEO support is vital as the program evolves to support new and changing needs.

6. The three ways the CEO can lead in digital transformation are:
    - Define priority areas where digital transformation will have the most impact or where there is the most need for change.
    - Drive and choreograph organizational change, and the capabilities and processes that support it.
    - Empower people at all levels and across all parts of the organization through pervasive access to information.

7. The correct answer choice is A.

8. The CEO can push IT to reorient away from traditional approaches and structures toward a focus on information rather than data. CEOs can promote data science and analytics and ensure that change sticks amid market disruptions and evolving business priorities.

9. The correct answer choice is D.

10. Given the inclusion of data governance and the utilization of data as an asset, the role of the data manager falls under the direction of the CDO. In complex organizations, data managers, as subordinates of the CDO, may be assigned to different business lines to focus on data management and deliver value from information from the unit's perspective.

11. The four archetypes of Chief Data Officer leaders and areas of responsibility are:
    - Governance
    - Operations
    - Innovation
    - Analytics.

12. The following are the functions of the Chief Digital Officer (CXO).
    - Map digital capabilities to strategic priorities.
    - Serve as the executive sponsor for digital process innovation.
    - Develop and administer the digital project portfolio.
    - Measure new efficiencies and return on investment.
    - Develop ways to attract and retain top digital transformation talent.
    - Be the "executive intermediary" during delivery.

13. CIOs focus on automating existing processes, delivering legacy business models and internal operations and functions, optimizing delivery of offerings and systems of record, centralizing or outsourcing IT capability, and reducing costs, often by moving to the cloud. CXOs emphasize transforming business processes, creating new—often customer facing—digital business models, optimizing the digital experience and systems of engagement (with customers), and decentralizing or democratizing data and process, primarily in the cloud.

14. The correct answer choice is B.

15. While both have an interest in data, digital transformation has an end date, although often in the distant future, so the CXO's role will end. The CDO's role and responsibility will continue after the digital transformation is complete.

16. The challenges to implementing a digital business include:
    - The enterprise-wide nature and focus on information demand a cross-functional approach to definition and delivery.
    - The speed of change and the flexibility required in technology delivery call for new ways of working within IT.

17. The CoE approach combines long-term vision, political and organizational aptitude, and careful day-to-day management over multiple years to enable digital transformation to succeed.

18. The skill set needed by the staff of the DBCoE includes:
    - Technical skills associated with their roles.
    - Political astuteness.

- A deep understanding of how to achieve goals through diplomacy, negotiation, and compromise.
- An understanding of the specific culture of the organization.

19. The responsibilities and roles of the digital business center of excellence (DBCoE) include:
    - Strategy setting, evolution, and linking to corporate business strategy.
    - Program design and ongoing management.
    - Business liaison and promotion.
    - Education, training, and support.
    - Design authority—information and function.
    - Liaison with Enterprise and Information Architecture, Data Governance, and similar groups.

20. The statement is True.

21. The DBCoE role in program design and ongoing management is to:
    - Develop and maintain the Staged Implementation Roadmap.
    - Support C-level management with details of project prioritization between business units, IT, data management, and other cross-enterprise initiatives.
    - Resolve conflicts between projects related to infrastructure and business deliverables.

22. The DBCoE plays a leading role in selling digital transformation across the business by:
    - Running regular informational and promotional meetings/events with management and senior staff.
    - Delivering internal marketing materials.
    - Sharing digital transformation success stories.

23. DBCoE's role in educating and training to support digital transformation includes:
    - Developing and delivering stakeholder and user education about digital business and DISA.
    - Developing and sharing information on data governance and policies related to current trends, such as data socialization and democratization, to support the concept of everyone being a data citizen.
    - Contributing to onboarding materials, newsletters, blogs, and town hall meetings.

24. The statement is False. The DBCoE ensures two-way communication between enterprise- and functional-level groups responsible for architecture and governance.

25. In contrast to traditional IT, which focuses on delivering and maintaining stable, reliable systems to support business-critical operations, digital transformation demands significant ongoing increases in the flexibility and speed of delivering new or improved functions and information to the business as the market and customer needs change.

26. Mode 1 is optimized for areas that are more predictable and well-understood. Mode 2 is exploratory, experimenting to solve new problems, and is optimized for areas of uncertainty.

27. The characteristics of Mode 1 include:
    - **Focus**: Enabling predictability, scalability, risk aversion, and cost savings while driving industrialization of services.
    - **Goal**: Stability.
    - **Culture**: IT-Centric.

- **Customer Proximity**: Remote from customer.
- **Trigger**: Performance and security improvement.
- **Value**: Performance of services.
- **Focus of Service**: Security and reliability.
- **Approach**: Waterfall development.
- **Application**: Systems of record or operational systems.
- **Speed of Service Delivery**: Slow.

28. The characteristics of Mode 2 include:
    - **Goal**: Agility and Speed.
    - **Culture**: Business-centric.
    - **Customer Proximity**: Close to the customer.
    - **Trigger**: Short-term market trend.
    - **Value**: Business moments, customer-branding.
    - **Focus of Service**: Innovation.
    - **Approach**: Iterative, Agile development.
    - **Application**: Systems of engagement.
    - **Speed of Service Delivery**: Fast.

29. This interdependence arises from the data shared and/or transferred between the two environments. New requirements arising from changing customer or market needs may be quickly and agilely addressed via Mode 2 methods until, of course, some update to the system of record is required, when slower and more careful Mode 1 methods would come into play, slowing down the Mode 2 gallop.

30. The DBCoE is responsible for identifying and managing the interdependencies between the two teams, requiring a focus on planning detailed features and release timing. The DBCoE has knowledge of both the traditional system of record realities and planned changes, enabling successful planning for Mode 2 systems-of-engagement activities and project deliverables. The DBCoE synchronizes iterative delivery of Mode 2 product releases with the more slowly evolving capabilities of the systems of record.

31. The correct answer choice is A.

32. The ways information can be monetized directly or indirectly include:
    - Direct methods include selling, trading, and offering information products.
    - Indirect methods include analytics to improve performance, product development, and relationship management.

33. The correct answer choice is C.

34. Foundational measures improve the management information discipline. Measures include:
    - Intrinsic value of information (IVI), which measures how correct, complete, and scarce the data is.
    - Business value of information (BVI), which measures how good and relevant the data is for the specific purpose.
    - Performance value of information (PVI), which measures how the data relates to or affects key business drivers.

35. The correct answer choice is D.

36. With these measures, infonomics provides a formal approach to establishing and communicating the value of information to the enterprise and may be useful in creating the necessary cross-organizational acceptance of digital transformation plans and priorities.

37. Organizational issues in which there is a lack of coherence between people, process, information, and technology.

38. The statement is False. A strong data culture is the first step in equipping staff with the skills needed to leverage data and contribute to its valorization.

39. The three challenges to defining the information framework are:
    - **Fragmentation**: Information is spread over multiple different, possibly contradictory systems that must be assembled or integrated again and again as requirements change which leads to disparity of data definitions, questions of ownership, and ultimately decreasing usability over time.
    - **Volatility**: The opportunities technology offers businesses to interact and assemble their processes in different ways leads to volatility in the information landscape.
    - **Context switching**: Using information outside the context in which it was created is becoming the norm, leading to repeated questions about what a piece of information means and multiple answers depending on the circumstances of its use.

40. The three layers of the connected are human interaction, alignment, and information, which combine to answer the question of what to organize. Alignment governs both human interaction and information. Human interaction is supported by information and requires alignment.

41. Although these three roles are conceptually distinct, in practice, the same people may act in more than one role. This is especially true in smaller organizations. Data managers will need to recognize potential overlap and address the underlying alignment and information layers separately.

42. The connected architecture provides a framework that enables collaboration to facilitate incremental development. Everyone learns from collaboration and from inspecting the results, enabling changes to the landscape and the conditions for human interaction. The result is an incremental design that allows evolution as conditions and directions change.

43. Information consumers turn information into activities and decisions that deliver value to the organization. Information producers are the people who prepare the data and interpret the resulting information. This large group of data professionals, including data managers, provides a bridge between businesspeople and IT. They ensure maximum transfer of contextual information and minimal misunderstanding or loss, which is vital to succeeding in digital transformation.

System Development for Digital Business

Educational Objectives

Upon completion of this assignment, you should be able to:

1. Describe the challenges associated with information-centric systems delivery.
2. List the activities that comprise software development.
3. List the common development methodologies for software projects.
4. Describe the Waterfall Model and its strengths and weaknesses.
5. Describe the Agile Methodology and its strengths and weaknesses.
6. Describe the role and responsibilities of the Data Manager and Data Management team in the different software development lifecycle methodologies.
7. Explain the concepts of DevOps and DataOps and how they address the entire software development and deployment lifecycle.
8. Show the importance of a program approach to the implementation of DISA.
9. Describe the program components, including the initiation and proof-of-concept projects.
10. Explain the staged implementation roadmap and list its contents.

For each assignment, define or describe each of the Key Terms and Concepts and answer each of the Review and Discussion Questions.

Key Terms and Concepts

DevOps:

DataOps:

Staged Implementation Approach:

Staged implementation roadmap (SIR):

Review Questions

1) What business challenges have pushed enterprise systems to change, and how has IT traditionally responded?

2) Identify the activities that comprise software development.

3) Identify the common development methodologies for software projects.

4) How do these methodologies compare?

5) Describe the Waterfall Model of systems development.

6) How do developers address the criticism that the Waterfall Model flow is too rigid and one-directional?

7) Backflows can exist in the Waterfall Model in all the following situations except:
    A. From design to requirements, the design identifies conflicting or unimplementable business needs.
    B. From implementation to design-as-code, testing discovers design flaws.
    C. During maintenance, account for new requirements.
    D. From verification to requirements, testing identifies missing business needs.

8) Which of the other system development methods attempts to preserve the engineering strengths of the Waterfall Model while introducing more agility and iteration?

9) Why are Waterfall and similar methodologies not generally applied to digital transformation programs?

10) True or False? The Agile method is less flexible and iterative than the Waterfall model.

11) Describe the Agile method.

12) List the steps in the Agile Methodology.

13) What are the strengths of the Agile approach?

14) What are the weakness of the Agile method?

15) True or False? Agile and related methodologies are well-suited to the velocity and changeability demands of digital transformation.

16) What is the role of the data manager in the systems development process?

17) How might the data manager support the planning function in systems development?

18) Which of the following is true of the data manager's role in systems development?
   A. Data Managers support the requirements gathering function in systems development by ensuring that business and IT begin with the same, enterprise-wide agreed data names, definitions, sources, code values, etc. (where they exist) as a common foundation for discussion and design.
   B. Data Managers support the architecture and design function in systems development by reviewing and validating that data flow diagrams, data models, and data mappings align with data management principles and best practices.
   C. Data Managers must engage in discussions about shortcuts or workarounds in data sourcing or consolidation to consider data quality impacts and cross-enterprise consistency.
   D. All of the above are true.

19) Which of the following is NOT true of the data manager's role in systems development?
   A. Data Managers support the architecture and design function in systems development by reviewing and validating data flow diagrams, data models, and data mappings to align with data management principles and best practices.
   B. Data Managers support the requirements-gathering function in systems development by ensuring that data quality rules and thresholds are encoded into the system and that monitoring mechanisms are put in place.
   C. Data Managers support the testing function in systems development by ensuring that the testing team can leverage the same development quality checks to reduce the number of data defects carried into production.
   D. Data Managers support the production function in systems development by monitoring data quality dashboards and alerts, warning businesspeople when thresholds they've set are breached, and partnering with business to determine why and what course of action should be taken.

20. How does DevOps support the entire software development lifecycle and how does that lead to better results for the enterprise?

21. All of the following are common traits indicative of successful DevOps adoption, except: [EO 7 P 9]
   A. Existing strong culture of collaboration and open communication.
   B. An executive leadership team that sees IT as a cost center.
   C. Sponsorship from a high enough level to allow challenges to the status quo.
   D. Applications built in-house and developed on open technologies.

22. How do DevOps and DataOps differ?

23. How does DataOps support data usage in an organization?

24. What is necessary for a successful DataOps approach?

25. In the staged implementation approach to data warehouse development, which of the following is NOT a major development area?
    A. **Customer analysis**: A review and analysis of current and potential customers to determine which data to include in the warehouse.
    B. **Business function**: A prioritized and agreed business need for a particular department or set of businesspeople, usually defined around the questions the users want answered or specific reporting requirements.
    C. **Enterprise modeling**: Parts of the overall enterprise data model that support the chosen business deliverable but are scoped in a broader view for subsequent reuse and expansion. This typically demands broadly based definitions of key entities in the initial stages, with consequently larger and longer initial projects in the program, but offers significant reuse in later, thus shorter, stages.
    D. **Infrastructure development**: Elements of common technology infrastructure required for this stage but capable of reuse and/or extension in later stages, such as a database; extract, transform, and load (ETL) function; or business intelligence (BI) tooling.

26. What are the three parts of the DISA Staged Implementation Program and how do these differ from the data warehouse application?

27. What steps are taken to ensure continuous oversight of the DISA Staged Implementation Program?

28. What activities are included in the initiation project of a DISA Staged Implementation Program?

29. Identify the three phases of the initiation program of a DISA Staged Implementation Program and their purposes.

30. What activities are included in Phase 1 of the initiation program of a DISA Staged Implementation Program?

31. What activities are included in Phase 2 of the initiation program of a DISA Staged Implementation Program?

32. What deliverables are the result of Phase 3 of the initiation program of a DISA Staged Implementation Program?

33. Describe the characteristics of the technology proof-of-concept (PoC) project.

34. Of the following, which is NOT true of the technology PoC project?
    A. A strength of the technology PoC approach is its ability to focus on a particular aspect of digital business implementation.
    B. A strength of the technology PoC approach is that it proves that all the parts of the system can work together.
    C. A strength of the technology PoC approach is proving the ability of IT personnel to deliver in this area, or testing a vendor's claims for their particular tool.
    D. A weakness of the technology PoC approach is that, because it delivers no business value, technology PoCs cannot provide a rationale for digital transformation.

35. All of the following are characteristics of the business proof-of-concept (PoC) project except:
    A. The business PoC focuses on delivering specific business value, usually at the expense of one or more aspects of the strategic DISA infrastructure.
    B. The requirements are reasonably well defined and the users are already supportive.
    C. The PoC uses both internal and external data to show the value of digital transformation.
    D. The driver for a business PoC is typically an urgent need for the delivery of a particular digital business application.

36. Of the following, which is NOT a weakness of the business proof-of-concept (PoC) project?
    A. The business PoC slows down PoC delivery because of the migration to strategic tools.
    B. Because the data scope is well defined in advance, a business PoC may conflict with the aim to address broad enterprise information considerations.
    C. The sources for this data may be multiple and varied, leading to potentially complex infrastructure needs and infrastructure compromises.

    D. Business PoCs are often subject to severe delivery pressure because the executives have committed to the business need before agreeing on the scope of the PoC project.

37. Which of the two types of proof-of-concept approaches is more likely to lead to a successful digital transformation? What is the optimal approach?

38. What is the purpose of the staged implementation roadmap (SIR)?

39. Key elements of the Staged Implementation Roadmap include:
    A. The outline of the IDEAL and REAL architectures describes them at a high level, as defined and adopted, and shows how they apply within the organization.
    B. Implications for existing and new systems allow the owners of existing systems to see how digital transformation will affect them and which areas will require investment in application changes or new infrastructure.
    C. Potential areas of benefit and possible cost, although not a cost/benefit analysis, provide a reasonable estimate of costs and some idea of potential benefits.
    D. All of the above are key elements.

40. **True or False?** A key element of the Stage Implementation Roadmap is a proposed organizational structure that shows the organization needed to drive the digital transformation, including the staff to involve.

41. What are the two levels of sign-off for the SIR?

Discussion Questions

NOTE: The questions below are intended to continue to challenge you to test your knowledge of the required reading by applying what you have studied to real-life situations.

1) What issues has your company faced in the development of a digital business?

2) What systems development methodologies are in use in your organization? What challenges have evolved from these methodologies?

Answers to Assignment 11 Questions

NOTE: These answers are provided to give students a basic understanding of acceptable types of responses. They are often not the only valid answers and are not intended to provide an exhaustive response to the questions.

Key Terms and Concepts

DevOps: A collection of principles, tools, and even culture that endeavors to unify the development of software and its implementation in operations, and allows faster and more reliable deployment of software.

DataOps: An application of DevOps thinking to the development and deployment of analytics and data-centric solutions. DataOps is the ability to enable solutions, develop data products, and activate data for business value across all technology tiers from infrastructure to experience.

Staged Implementation Approach: An enterprise-level solution to development, delivered through a program of related projects, each with defined business value over a period of a year. Initially developed for data warehouse applications but now used for DISA.

Staged implementation roadmap (SIR): This document outlines the overall shape of the program and the major implementation steps, provides the basis for executive approval of the rollout, and provides, for each area of the business, an initial view of how and when the program will meet their particular needs.

Review Questions

1) The business needs to know what is happening and what is changing so that appropriate actions can be taken to support it. Their systems need to change to provide executives and managers with the information they need to explore options, innovate analyses, obtain novel data, and retrieve new data from existing systems. IT modifies or extends the system at short notice, often with conflicting or multiple requirements. These changes can occur continuously in large, complex businesses, making it difficult to keep databases and warehouses responsive.

2) The activities that comprise software development are:
   - Problem analysis.
   - Market research into existing potential solutions.
   - Requirements gathering.
   - Planning the development.
   - Architecture and design of the software.
   - Implementation (coding).
   - Testing.

- Deployment.
- Operations support.
- Maintenance and bug fixing.

3) Common development methodologies for software projects include:
- Waterfall Model.
- V-Model.
- Spiral Model.
- Rational Unified Process Methodology (RUP).
- Joint Application Development Methodology.
- Feature-Driven Development (FDD).
- Agile Methodology.
- Scrum Development Methodology (often with Kanban).
- Rapid Application Development (RAD).
- Dynamic System Development.
- Lean Development Methodology.
- Extreme Programming (XP).
- DevOps Methodology.
- Prototype Methodology.
- Design Thinking.

4) The methodologies overlap to some extent and address different aspects of development. For some, the focus is on well-engineered software that accurately meets users' needs, which typically results in slower product delivery. For others, the need for fast delivery drives more iterative approaches, especially when combined with poorly defined or changing requirements. The result is that different methodologies are more suitable for different types of projects.

5) The Waterfall Model proceeds as a linear, sequential, downward flow of activities from problem analysis to maintenance. The emphasis is on well-understood, carefully documented requirements—agreed up-front between business and IT—and on formal transitions between the different stages of the process.

6) Most modern instantiations recognize that "backflows" are possible and often required across all levels; for example, from implementation to design, as code testing discovers design flaws, or from design back to requirements, when design identifies conflicting or unimplementable business needs.

7) The correct answer choice is C.

8) System development methods that attempt to preserve the engineering strengths of the Waterfall Model while introducing more agility and iteration include:
- V-Model.
- Spiral Model.
- Rational Unified Process Methodology (RUP).
- Joint Application Development Methodology.
- Feature-Driven Development (FDD).

9) In the context of digital business transformation, the Waterfall and related methodologies are less commonly encountered due to the extreme speed and flexibility requirements of digital transformation. In addition, digital business developers often come from open software or cloud development backgrounds; they are thus more comfortable with Agile approaches.

10) This statement is False. The Agile method is more flexible and iterative than the Waterfall model. Business is continuously involved in the project throughout its lifecycle, resulting in higher user satisfaction.

11) The methodology requires developers to start with a simple, compact project design and proceed with fast, incremental development sprints of small component modules, also known as product backlog items (PBIs). Within each sprint, a component is developed and tested within a time period as short as a week or a month. After completion of each sprint, the development team, including business users, evaluates the work with the "Scrum master," who is in overall charge, providing vital feedback and enabling rapid response to problems or changes in requirements. In addition, any bugs in the code are also analyzed and fixed.

12) The steps in the Agile Methodology are:
- The product owner develops a list of small components, known as product backlog items.
- The development team plans the work to accomplish the sprint goal.
- Work is organized into short periods, known as sprints, with daily meetings between the team and the scrum master to discuss progress, problems, and needs to refine the backlog.
- Testing occurs when components are produced.
- An incremental product is produced and released.
- The team meets for a scrum review and selects the next module from the backlog to develop, and the process starts again.

13) The Agile methodology delivers results quickly and is flexible to changes in business needs, which are discovered continuously through direct communication between businesspeople and developers. This method minimizes risk and increases customer satisfaction.

14) Agile lacks the strong initial design phase and comprehensive requirements documentation seen in the Waterfall Model. While speeding up the development, these lacks may lead to significant challenges in large, complex, interconnected systems. Although (or because) the method is highly adaptive to change, projects can easily get off track if users are not clear about their final goal. Future software extensions may also be affected by the lack of formal documentation.

15) This statement is True.

16) The role of the data manager in the development process is largely supervisory, ensuring data is secure, organized, governed, and fit for purpose. The data manager should understand where all data-related responsibilities lie and engage with the involved parties to ensure data is managed appropriately.

17) Data managers can help their organization understand which data roles will be needed on the project based on how the data is expected to be used. Use of critical data for compliance purposes or executive decision-making may require all or most of the data management disciplines; use of data for R&D purposes may

18) The correct answer choice is D.

19) The correct answer choice is B. Data Managers support the <u>development</u> function in systems development by ensuring that data quality rules and thresholds are encoded into the system and that monitoring mechanisms are put in place.

20) DevOps demands that programmers have ongoing involvement with their code throughout its operational lifetime, right to its end of life. Such involvement allows for faster, better fixes to problems or upgrades with new features. It also gives developers more insight into how their products are used in the business and, indeed, how the business operates in reality.

21) The correct answer choice is B.

22) DevOps focuses on the software development/deployment process, where data considerations are often an afterthought. DataOps puts data front and center in a process primarily aimed at supporting data scientists and data engineers in digital business.

23) DataOps starts from the concept of a data pipeline, an integrated series of steps that takes data from a source all the way to its business user, and aims to automate the process from concept through development and deployment to ongoing use by the business.

24) Management of data resources—everything from personal spreadsheets to centralized databases—in a digital business is a broader undertaking. CSI, a key source of information about where data is stored, its provenance and lineage, and even its meaning and use, is vital to the deployment of DataOps approaches.

25) The correct answer choice is A.

26) The three parts of the DISA Staged Implementation Program and how they differ from the data warehouse application are:
   - **Business function**: The business function may be operational or informational in scope, or a combination of both, so development constraints will differ accordingly.
   - **Information context**: The data needs of DISA are significantly broader and more varied than in the data warehouse application, with valid trade-offs to be made between data consistency and timeliness, different levels and types of structure and context, and the scope of reliance/usage required.
   - **REAL Infrastructure**: The scope of DISA also leads to broader considerations in this element, but the underlying motivation remains the same: to build the necessary infrastructure incrementally and consistently for this and subsequent projects.

27) In advance of the program roll-out, the initial work consists of an initiation and proof-of-concept (PoC) phase, which is followed by the development of the key management tool for the program, the staged implementation roadmap (SIR).

28) The following activities are included in the initiation project of a DISA Staged Implementation Program:
   - The promoter of digital business transformation must gain acceptance of the overall business justification for the entire approach.
   - If this is the company's first use of information modeling or data quality management, establishing a support structure for these activities may be necessary.
   - New organizational structures to promote cooperation between different areas of the business and between business and IT may need to be established.
   - A new approach to the justification and prioritization of IT development must be established to enable subsequent steps.
   - New infrastructure components and sources (for example, open-source and/or cloud) may require new management and procurement processes.
   - The teams responsible for implementing the first step need education and training.

29) The three phases of the initiation program of a DISA Staged Implementation Program and their purposes are:
- **Phase 1**: Initial education and orientation is designed to reach consensus on what digital business, etc., means for your organization, what such a strategy seeks to achieve, and to enable concerted action in the initiation project.
- **Phase 2**: Requirements definition and high-level modeling are designed to discover and document the broad business requirements that will drive the entire digital transformation process.
- **Phase 3**: Long-term planning and Proof of Concept initiation is designed to gain business approval and commitment to the DISA-staged implementation program, and to demonstrate that it can deliver both business value and DISA infrastructure.

30) The activities included in Phase 1 of the initiation program of a DISA Staged Implementation Program are:
- Initial exploration of and education on digital business.
- Obtaining the necessary management approval to proceed.
- Building and educating the initiation and extended teams responsible for the initiation project.

31) The activities included in Phase 2 of the initiation program of a DISA Staged Implementation Program are:
- Requirements definition.
- High-level information context.

32) The deliverables that are the result of Phase 3 of the initiation program of a DISA Staged Implementation Program include:
- Customized DISA architecture of the generic conceptual and logical architectures, adapted to the specific environment of the company. It also identifies the tools or development needed to build it.
- Staged implementation roadmap (SIR).
- Proof-of-concept (PoC) plan and high-level design that demonstrate IT's ability to deliver digital transformation.

33) The technology PoC is the simplest for IT and also the least useful in moving the digital business forward. Its purpose is to allow IT to prove the technical viability of the tools to be used in the production implementation. Typical technology PoCs include prototyping a new database system, demonstrating streaming technology, or implementing an initial cloud solution—each using only a minimal set of sample data.

34) The correct answer choice is B.

35) The correct answer choice is C.

36) The correct answer choice is A.

37) A business PoC is more likely to cement the success of digital transformation than a pure technology PoC, simply because it delivers visible business value. The ideal, of course, is to find a balance between the two extremes to show some reasonable business value and prove the underpinning technology.

38) The purpose of the staged implementation roadmap is to provide an overarching, conceptual plan for implementing a digital business in accordance with the DISA. It provides the entire enterprise with a view of what digital business is, its benefits, how it would affect the organization in general, and a flavor of how it could be delivered. SIR is an internal marketing brochure that provides a vision of the digital transformation to be implemented and an assurance that it can be.

39) The correct answer choice is D.

40) This statement is False.

41) The two levels of sign-off for the SIR are:
- The overall sign-off accepts the structure and approach of the roadmap, in particular that the putative roll-out in section 8 is subject to regular review and revision as business and market conditions change, as technology evolves, and as projects meet or fail to meet expectations in deliverables or timeframes.
- The sign-off of section 9, Project 1, is a formal, cross-organizational commitment to this project, its scope, deliverables, and delivery schedule.

Ethical Considerations for Digital Business

Educational Objectives

Upon completion of this assignment, you should be able to:

1. Discuss how data-usage risks emerge in a big-data-driven business.
2. Describe how data-driven decision making can adversely impact insurance.
3. Explain how big data and AI impact privacy.
4. Identify and describe techniques to address surveillance capitalism, social justice, and discrimination that can result from excessive digital transformation.
5. Discuss bias in data, algorithms, and indeed humans.
6. Discuss how ethical hazards can be avoided or overcome in the areas of privacy and bias.
7. Explain the drives toward automation and augmentation, and why the former is favored.
8. Discuss how automation may disrupt employment and the possible consequences for the economy.
9. Describe data ethics and explain how it can be embedded in business.

For each assignment, define or describe each of the Key Terms and Concepts and answer each of the Review and Discussion Questions.

Key Terms and Concepts

E-scores:

Privacy:

Informational Privacy:

Obscurity in Privacy Theory:

Surveillance Capitalism:

Anonymization:

Privacy by Design (PbD):

Explainable AI (XAI):

Information Complexity:

Problem Complexity:

Data Ethics:

Review Questions

1) How does using process-mediated data (PMD) to support management decision making increase business risk?

2) How has the explosion of big data, both externally sourced machine-generated and human-sourced data, transformed how the business interacts with its customers?

3) An example of the social consequences of poor decisions includes:
   A. When poor data leads to incorrect pricing and reduced profit, the company may reduce staffing.
   B. Data problems and poor decisions in government agencies can lead to the loss of services for the needy.
   C. Insurance companies may overestimate premium payments for certain groups, making insurance unaffordable in some cases.
   D. All of the above can be consequences of poor decision-making.

4) What is the role of actuarial science in the insurance marketplace and how has big data affected this role?

5) What is the potential problem with the use of big data in actuarial analyses?

6) True or False? Use of segmentation generated through insurers' proprietary and confidential algorithms and based on a range of socioeconomic measures may develop premiums that have little to do with how well one drives.

7) How may the use of e-scores, such as credit ratings, drive a feedback loop that makes it harder for certain groups to purchase automobile insurance?

8) How can pay-as-you-drive insurance improve on the use e-scores to segment the automobile insurance market?

9) Pay-as-you-drive:
    A. Completely predicts and prices risk at the individual level.
    B. May improve profit margins but runs contrary to the principle of pooling risk.
    C. Encourages high-risk drivers to use the methodology to reduce their premiums.
    D. All of the above.

10) What role can data managers play in identifying the ethics of data usage?

11) List the attributes of informational privacy.

12) All of the government approaches to address privacy issues except:
    A. Health Insurance Portability and Accountability Act (HIPAA).
    B. California's Consumer Privacy Act (CPA).
    C. Supreme Court ruling in Anderson v. United States.
    D. NAIC (National Association of Insurance Commissioners) Insurance Information and Privacy Protection Model Law and NAIC Artificial Intelligence Guiding Principles.

13) What does safe mean in terms of obscurity in privacy theory? How has big data and the powerful search engines affected obscurity?

14) How do traditional businesses contrast with complete digital businesses and how is traditional business changing?

15) Identify techniques of anonymization.

16) True or False? Deanonymization is a significant threat because so many data attributes are stored about most people. As a result, it is not overlooked during development efforts.

17) How does privacy by design (PbD) differ from anonymization?

18) What are the principles of privacy by design (PbD)?

19) Why is minimizing the volume of data important for both data management and efficiency?

20) Common causes of bias include all of the following except:
    A. Bias within common data sources.
    B. Algorithms embed beliefs and motivations.
    C. Technology errors.
    D. Interaction-driven bias.

21) Provide an example of bias within common data sources.

22) How might bias be introduced within algorithms?

23) What concept is fundamental to judging and reducing bias? Why is it such a complicated concept to understand? How does this affect AI?

24) Why is a high level of explainability, traceability, and fairness necessary for insurance AI systems?

25) Suggestions offered to maximize fairness and reduce bias in AI do NOT include:
   A. Establishment of processes and practices to test functionality.
   B. Awareness of the contexts in which AI can help correct for bias, as well as where there is a high risk that AI could exacerbate bias.
   C. Engaging in fact-based conversations about potential biases in human decisions.
   D. Fully exploring how humans and machines can work best together.

26) What should be considered at different levels within the organization to address potential impacts of data and algorithms?

27) Identify and describe the fundamental factors involved in augmentation and automation.

28) How does the combination of information and problem complexity map to different decision-making tools?

29) Describe the situations where automation and augmentation can be applied to improve decision-making.

30) Why is automation favored over augmentation? What is the ethical concern with this approach?

31) Where do data managers stand in the debate on ethical concerns?

32) Where does ethical data management originate from in an organization?

33) Describe the areas of concern when discussing data ethics.

34) Common data ethical issues include:
   A. Transparency and personal responsibility for the goals and intents of AI programs and algorithm use.
   B. Transparency in the choices of data used for training and their sourcing, and in the overall quality and fitness for purpose.
   C. Obscurity of models used and the inference approaches applied.
   D. Systematic benchmarking of the chosen methods.

35) What are the principles of the Code of Ethics and Professional Conduct?

Discussion Questions

NOTE: The questions below are intended to continue to challenge you to test your knowledge of the required reading by applying what you have studied to real-life situations.

1)   What ethical concerns has your organization been struggling with as it moves to a digital business?

2)   How has your organization addressed any ethical concerns? Who leads the effort?

Answers to Assignment 12 Questions

NOTE: These answers are provided to give students a basic understanding of acceptable types of responses. They are often not the only valid answers and are not intended to provide an exhaustive response to the questions.

Key Terms and Concepts

E-scores: Socioeconomic segmentation, often based on hundreds of measures including credit history, use of department-store or bank credit cards, and even TV provider.

Privacy: Freedom from interference or intrusion; Everyone has a sphere of existence and activity that properly belongs to them alone, where they should be free of constraint, coercion, and uninvited observation.

Informational Privacy: The right to control access to personal information.

Obscurity in Privacy Theory: The idea that information is safe—at least to some degree—when it is hard to obtain and/or understand.

Surveillance Capitalism: A form of capitalism where data is simply an asset to be monetized, irrespective of undesirable outcomes for society or moral hazards.

Anonymization: Protecting private or sensitive information by erasing or encrypting identifiers, such as names, social security numbers, and addresses, that identify an individual.

Privacy by Design (PbD): A framework that can form a strong basis for decisions and action when acquiring and using any data with PII characteristics.

Explainable AI (XAI): An emerging field that inspects and tries to understand the steps and models involved in [AI systems] making decisions.

Information Complexity: A judgment about how easy or difficult it is to understand, analyze, and trust the information on which a decision is based.

Problem Complexity: Involves judgment about where on the deterministic/ambiguous axis a problem falls.

Review Questions

1. Using PMD to support management decision making in increases the demands made on the quality and cross-functional consistency of the data, as well as usability and understandability by businesspeople. These demands place new responsibilities on business and IT, as well as increasing

the need for data management to consider the impact of data quality on decisions made using this data.

2. Traditional business decision making applies largely at a collective level. Traditional business is content to record a sale in PMD and measure profit by product line. Digital business decisions directly and continuously affect individuals. The digital business wants to understand from detailed HSI and MGD why the product was bought and instead of what, how it is used, and how this captured behavior can influence this person and their acquaintances to buy more.

3. The correct answer choice is D.

4. Actuarial science has enabled insurers to estimate the likelihood of accidents, deaths, or fires within large groups of people. Big data analytics enable more granular risk segmentation, which can be an important contributor to an insurance carrier's profitability and survival, as well as an attractive feature for prospective customers.

5. The data used may be chosen based on greater ready availability and ease of analysis than on a direct relationship to the risk involved. Correlation is easily followed in machine learning, while causation is often overlooked.

6. The statement is True.

7. Positive feedback loops develop when the use of credit scores can lead to higher premiums for the poor. With higher premiums, more of the poor will default, lowering their credit score and thus raising their premiums.

8. For the insurer, pay-as-you-drive data can allow for market segmentation based on a customer's driving history. For the insured, it also offers the promise of a personalized premium that can be influenced by changes in behavior.

9. The correct answer choice is B.

10. As those closest to the data being collected, its sources and quality, and the type of processing being applied, data managers have a special responsibility to examine how data is being used or misused. The ethical question to be answered is where the benefits and costs accrue. Is business profitability the sole measure of success, or do potential societal harms need to be considered?

11. The attributes of informational privacy are:
    - It is about information. It focuses on the quest for knowledge about someone rather than, say, physical proximity, constraint, or any other type of interference.
    - It refers to personal information. The knowledge intended provides some access to the subject's person, whether their identity, thoughts, aspirations, passions, habits, foibles, or transgressions.
    - The issue is one of control. It is not how much or how little is known about the subject, but whether the subject can choose how much of the information is revealed and to whom.
    - It is defined as a right. Within certain "domains," the person's control of personal information ought to be respected and protected.

12. The correct answer choice is C.

13. Safe in this context doesn't mean inaccessible, but rather that obtaining it demands competent and determined data hunting armed with the best tools. The advent of big data and search engines has made it easier to obtain data and thus reduced obscurity.

14. In the traditional business model, profits and growth are built primarily on physical resources, while in the modern, completely (or nearly so) digital businesses rely on the personal data they collect from their users—and, often, their children, friends, and even distant online acquaintances—as raw material. Traditional businesses are increasingly becoming dependent on such data as a key resource as they undertake digital transformation journeys.

15. Techniques of anonymization include:
    - Data masking: hiding data with characters such as **** or ####.
    - Data swapping: shuffling attribute values between records.
    - Data perturbation: modifying data slightly by rounding numbers and adding random noise.
    - Generalization: modifying data into ranges (e.g., deleting house number from an address).
    - Pseudonymization: replacing private identifiers with fake identifiers or pseudonyms.
    - Synthetic data: algorithmically manufacturing data that has no connection to real events.

16. The statement is False.

17. Anonymization is applied to individual data elements. Privacy by design (PbD) calls for privacy to be taken into account throughout the whole software engineering process, covering IT systems, accountable business practices, and physical design and networked infrastructure.

18. The principles of privacy by design (PbD) are:
    - Proactive, not Reactive; Preventative, not Remedial.
    - Privacy as the Default Setting.
    - Privacy Embedded into Design.
    - Full Functionality—Positive-Sum, not Zero-Sum.
    - End-to-End Security—Full Lifecycle Protection.
    - Visibility and Transparency—Keep it Open.
    - Respect for User Privacy—Keep it User-Centric.
    - Minimize, and then minimize again, the volume of data you acquire and use.

19. Even in big data analytics, return on investment begins to plateau as more detailed and granular data is analyzed. Furthermore, gradually increasing data acquisition volumes over time enables early recognition of data that is seldom used, reducing new acquisitions and focusing on deleting data that is no longer needed.

20. The correct answer choice is C.

21. Examples of bias within common data sources include:
    - Facial recognition can be skewed by imbalances in the proportion of photos of people of color, minorities, and the disabled among training data.
    - Law enforcement and parole algorithms can perpetuate racial discrimination based on training data compiled from prior biased human decisions.

22. Bias might be introduced within algorithms in the following ways:
    - Education, social welfare, and lending algorithms may be distorted due to unconscious beliefs, ideology, discredited research, and other influences.

- The choice of measures may drive algorithmic behavior in unexpected ways.
- Algorithms designed to learn continuously from real-world interactions can be influenced or gamed to reflect particular points of view or biases.
- Search algorithms contain inbuilt biases both deliberately to conform to societal norms and inadvertently as they adapt to evolving corpora of questions and answers.
- Filter bubbles drive heavily biased social media interactions and create search algorithm bias.
- Language contains inherent prejudices. People's names and language often correlate to gender, ethnicity, marital status, and even age, allowing bias to creep into AI algorithms in unexpected ways.

23. Fairness is fundamental to judging bias, but its meaning varies across cultures and time periods. While AI can reduce subjective interpretation of data by learning to consider only variables that improve predictive accuracy, fairness cannot be built into the algorithm. This necessitates human judgment to ensure AI-supported decision-making is fair.

24. In insurance, AI systems can have significant financial implications for customers. Therefore, insurers need to be able to explain why a decision was made. Furthermore, regulators may pay close attention to pricing and market fairness and require objective explanations of any changes.

25. The correct answer choice is A.

26. The potential impacts of data and algorithmic bias first demand deliberation at the board level when new AI initiatives are considered. Principles from sociology, psychology, and philosophy must be understood and applied in an attempt to consider the responses of individuals and society to pervasive algorithmic decision making. At lower organizational levels, experienced and skilled statisticians and data scientists should help determine which algorithms are useful and valid and when they should be implemented.

27. The fundamental factors involved in augmentation and automation are:
- Information complexity relates to the concepts on the structure/context axis of the information thinking space, distinguishing between hard data (limited in scope and easily manipulated mathematically) and soft information (with subtle meaning and, at best, only statistically analyzable). Usage and consistency aspects from the other two axes of the information space are also in play.
- Problem complexity refers to where a problem falls on the deterministic/ambiguous scale. In the pure deterministic case, simple logic or math leads from the information available to a single answer. As problems become more ambiguous, background knowledge and judgment must be applied.

28. Highly deterministic problems with good, hard data inputs can be handled by traditional operational applications with very specific, hard-coded rules. Business intelligence offers greater flexibility in decision-making at the expense of increased algorithmic complexity. This trend continues through analytic tools and machine learning as problems become more ambiguous and data becomes softer.

29. Automation is most easily applied to deterministic problems and increasing its algorithmic complexity is most easily applied to handling softer information inputs. The growing collection of big data offers opportunities for ever greater automation. Augmentation is most appropriate for ambiguous problems, where human judgment is generally needed to assess possible and even

unexpected outcomes. In such cases, additional data/information may contribute only minimal additional clarity on outcomes.

30. Increasing automation is strongly driven by financial considerations. Eliminating human involvement can significantly reduce operating costs and speed up actions. Augmentation retains strong but costly elements of human discretion. The ethical concern is that complex statistical algorithms are often used to automate rather than augment decisions that affect human health, income, privacy, and other fundamental rights or needs.

31. Data managers stand at a key intersection point between business and information technology, between data without context and information contextualized by how it is collected and used, between analytics for profit alone and its use for the wider good.

32. While some technology solutions exist, data management ethics begin at the level of personal and organizational norms and behavior.

33. The areas of concern when discussing data ethics include:
    - **Data Handling**: Generation, recording, curation, processing, dissemination, sharing, and use.
    - **Algorithms**: AI, artificial agents, machine learning, and robots.
    - Corresponding Practices: responsible innovation, programming, hacking, and professional codes.

34. The correct answer choice is C.

35. The principles of the Code of Ethics and Professional Conduct include:
    - Contribute to society and to human well-being, acknowledging that all people are stakeholders in computing.
    - Avoid harm.
    - Be honest and trustworthy.
    - Be fair and take action not to discriminate.
    - Respect the work required to produce new ideas, inventions, creative works, and computing artifacts.
    - Respect privacy.
    - Honor confidentiality.